OPTIMAL THINKING

How to enjoy the best life has to offer

Rosalene Glickman, repeatedly honoured by the media as 'Australia's most successful woman', shares the secrets of her success. Chief Executive Officer of The World Academy of Personal Development in Beverly Hills, California and Toorak, Melbourne, her Optimal strategies have been adopted by numerous organisations including Mercedes-Benz, National Australia Bank, Warner Bros., Touche Ross and The Australian Society of Accountants. She was recently nominated for the Order of Australia. Rosalene hosts the television program 'The Joys of Living' where she helps others discover their best formulae for success.

OPTIMAL THINKING

How to enjoy the best life has to offer

ROSALENE GLICKMAN

The World Academy of Personal Development Inc.
449 S. Beverly Drive, Suite 214, Beverly Hills, CA 90212
Tel: (310) 557-2761   Fax: (310) 557-2762
info@optimalthinking.com
www.optimalthinking.com

SIMON & SCHUSTER

AUSTRALIA

DEDICATION

To my beloved parents,
Sarah and Joseph Glickman.
In appreciation of all your love and support.

OPTIMAL THINKING

First published in Australasia in 1990
by Simon & Schuster Australia
7 Grosvenor Place, Brookvale NSW 2100

Reprinted 1990

A division of Paramount Communications Inc.
Sydney   New York   London   Toronto   Tokyo

National Library of Australia
Cataloguing in Publication data
Glickman, Rosalene
Optimal thinking: how to enjoy the best life has to offer.

Includes index.
ISBN 0 7318 0103 2

1. Creative thinking. 2. Creative ability in business.
3. Success in business. I. Title.

153.42

Designed by Jack Jagtenberg
Cartoons by Greg Gaul

Typeset in Australia by The Type Shop

Printed in Australia by The Book Printer

Contents

ACKNOWLEDGEMENTS

It is my greatest pleasure to acknowledge:

My family and friends, Sarah and Joseph Glickman, Janet Fust, Jeffrey and Michael, Morry, Sarah, Andrew and Tammy for all their love and support. My beloved friend, Halina Margan, has lovingly supported me through life's challenges for almost two decades. Danial Wong, is an Optimal example of love and generosity.

Brian Jacobson, Beverly Marmor, Suzanne Moran, Eilleen Steinberg, Trishia Rust, Haim Eldan, Vicki Masters, Elaine Fidel, Shelley Faden, and Marlene Stern, thank you for all you have done to support me in being the best I can be.

I am most appreciative of the encouragement and Optimal feedback I have received from my publisher, Kirsty Melville, and my editor, Elenie Poulos, whose brilliant input optimised the structure and content of the book. To those who worked behind the scenes at Simon & Schuster, thank you.

My gratitude to Jane Elliott and Leanne Renfree for their Optimal input into the book and our computer based products, Dr Pat Allen, Elizabeth Upton, Marilyn Winfield, Marvin Wolf, SuSu Levy and Howard Usher, for their brilliant professional guidance, Paul J. Meyer, John and Jan Usher and Dr Barbara DeAngelis, for helping me and countless others.

Shelley Faden and Joseph Barth, Executive Producers, of my television show, *The Joys of Living*, and the production teams at American Cablesystems and Century Southwest Cable, deserve the highest praise. To Dr Earl Mindell, Dottie Walters, James Newman, Dr Morton Cooper, Irwin Zucker and the numerous guests who have appeared on *The Joys of Living*, and all the viewers, thank you for supporting the show.

My corporate clients and seminar participants deserve the utmost appreciation. Without you, Optimal Thinking would never have been tried, tested and proven.

CHAPTER ONE

OPTIMAL THINKING™

Do you enjoy the best life has to offer or are you stuck with a life of compromise and substitutes?

Optimal Thinking is for those who wish to be their best and enjoy the best life has to offer! It is for those who know that thought is creative and who are willing to optimise their lives by optimising their thinking!

Many people would love to enjoy Optimal relationships but find themselves in and out of unsatisfactory liaisons. Some want to make the most of their professional lives, but feel they are only making reasonable progress. They dream of all the rewards of financial success, yet are restricted by tight budgets. Others are overworked, trapped in the wrong jobs and unfulfilled at home.

This book does not attempt to give you specific solutions, but offers an approach which enables you to discover the best answers for yourself. You learn to ask yourself and others the best questions to make the most of everyday situations. You learn a style of thinking which provides you with the best chance of having everything you want.

Picture yourself involved in an activity where you feel totally resourceful, capable and confident. You may wish to direct your attention toward the simple process of breathing. Relax into the feeling of total mastery. Think about all the things in your life that encourage you to feel completely competent and confident. Now focus on your greatest blessings. Reflect on what you like most about yourself, your environment and life. You can choose to surround yourself with your favourite people and enjoy your favourite music. Decide what you want to see, hear, think and feel. Now imagine you are receiving your greatest desire.

YOU can exercise the full power of your positive thinking potential whenever you want!

You have, I'm sure, experienced almost all forms of thinking before picking up this book. Are you aware of your current thought mix? How much do you identify with the following thinking profiles?

NEGATIVE THINKING

Do you ever find yourself thinking negatively about yourself, others and experiences? Do you use fault-finding, fear, worry, blame and other forms of detrimental thinking? Do you frequently complain and use words like 'can't' and 'won't'? Are you ever unreasonable? Do you direct your anger at people who have nothing to do with its cause or solution?

We have all thought negatively at some time or another. We concentrate on fears, limitations and destructive viewpoints, and sabotage opportunities for success. Negative thinkers often squash new ideas or ventures. They are quick to point out exactly why they won't work. They prefer to focus on why things *can't* be done rather than how they *can* be done. In fact if you give them time, they will offer you numerous examples of failures in order to substantiate their arguments.

Negative thinkers are usually unhappy wherever they are. They often believe the grass is greener elsewhere. They forget that the grass turns green where they water it.

Does this describe you? How much of your time do you think negatively?

POSITIVE THINKING

Are you a positive thinker? Are you confident and assured? Is your thinking constructive and productive? When there's a problem, do you look for a solution? Do you think in terms of victory and success? Positive thinkers concentrate on the value in themselves, others and the world. They look for ways things can be done. They enthusiastically approach life with a 'can do' and 'will do' attitude, viewing failures as opportunities to learn and grow. Positive thinkers see themselves as good, loving, wise, competent and worthy of life's favourable offerings.

Heather, an aspiring actress in her early forties, was a positive thinker. She was convinced that her age would help, rather than hinder her to find success. She took acting lessons from well-regarded teachers and zealously refined her craft. She approached each day optimistically and auditioned for roles whenever she could. For Heather, each audition provided an opportunity to learn and grow. She developed confidence in herself as a good actress and persisted through numerous temporary setbacks, believing that success would soon be hers. One day she was offered an important role in a high budget film. She excelled in that role and went on to become a respected and highly successful actress.

Positive thinking is a necessary ingredient for success whether that success be mediocre, extraordinary or Optimal in nature. How much of your time do you invest in positive thinking?

INEFFECTIVE THINKING

Are you an ineffective thinker? Do you think in fruitless or unproductive terms? Ineffective thinkers are often devoid of purpose or incapable of achieving their purpose. They may even involve themselves in activities which are of no value to themselves and others. Their style of thinking is unproductive and unprofitable.

Edward was the top athlete in his division eighteen months ago. Since then he had suffered a traumatic divorce. His self-confidence and performance had been severely affected. His athletic activities had become fruitless. Edward had recently been rejected by the division's selection committee. He was feeling purposeless and ineffective.

After listening to Edward talk about his feelings of inadequacy and worthlessness, his friend Bob said, 'Edward, you have already been recognised as the top athlete in your division. You have got what it takes!' Edward replied ineffectively, 'I hope so'.

Is this you? How often is your thinking ineffective?

EFFECTIVE THINKING

Are you an effective thinker? Are you able to create the results you want? Do you know how to experience success in your field of work and other endeavours? Do you think of yourself as efficient and competent?

You are probably self-confident because you experience your personal power through your thinking. You can be effective in a negative, ineffective, positive, mediocre, extraordinary or Optimal way, depending on the nature of your thinking. Take the following examples.

Last year four members of the sales department of a successful automobile company discussed their aspirations for the following year. Roger, an extraordinarily positive thinker, was convinced that he would better his exceptional results of the previous year. Elizabeth, a mediocre thinker, said she would do a good job and take home a reasonable pay cheque to supplement her husband's salary. Earl, a senior salesperson, said it would be acceptable to him if he did not achieve a profit or make any headway during the year. He had other things on his mind. Betty was angry with the sales manager for divulging to others a personal matter and swore that she would make him pay for it. She was determined to make his life a misery.

At the beginning of this year the four members of the sales team had confirmed their effectiveness by unequivocally and proficiently achieving what they had set out to do. Roger had been effective in his extraordinarily positive way, Elizabeth had been effective in her mediocre way, Earl had been effective at being ineffective and Betty had efficiently achieved her negative goals.

Are you an effective thinker? If so, what percentage of your time is invested in effective thinking?

MEDIOCRE THINKING

Are you a mediocre thinker? When people ask you how you are, do you answer with words like 'not bad', 'OK', and 'pretty good'? Do you feel comfortable being considered average in your thinking and actions? Do you see yourself as the average or regular person? Would you describe your thinking as moderate and conventional?

Nora, a charming, good-hearted woman owns a modest home, drives a modest car and lives a seemingly comfortable life. She is convinced that she has no right to enjoy the best things in life. Although she has some extraordinary dreams, she has no faith in their fulfilment. She believes that the objects of her desires are unattainable or don't exist. It is obvious that her mediocre thinking began early in life. Her parents had constantly denigrated her intellect, behaviour and aspirations. She was continually reminded that she couldn't have what she wanted, and must compromise. She still fears taking actions which evoke disapproval from her family. Disgruntled with her life, at forty-four years of age she has not overcome her early negative conditioning.

You may be a positive thinker yet your thinking could still be mediocre. Do you consider yourself quite good at your job? Are you a pretty good family person, friend, or sports person? Is your thinking rarely offensive and do you feel comfortable being one of the crowd?

Do you identify with this description? How much of your time do you devote to mediocre thinking?

EXTRAORDINARY THINKING

What of extraordinary thinking? Is this you? Do you think in terms of being more than ordinary, unusually great, exceptional? Do you like to think beyond the realms of mediocrity? Do you like to challenge the limited thinking of most people? Do words like 'excellent', 'brilliant', 'outstanding', and 'high achiever' describe you?

The Chief Executive Officer of a large and successful corporation recently came to me for a personal consultation. He responded to the question 'What is the primary purpose of your company?' with 'To create exceptionally high returns for our shareholders' as part of an overall statement. He was an extraordinary thinker.

Many people are empowered by their refusal to give in to seemingly unsurpassable limitations and obstacles. Thomas Edison invented the electric light bulb when all around him believed it wasn't possible. He succeeded after 10 000 attempts. When asked about all the unsuccessful attempts, he stated: 'I didn't fail. I just discovered another way not to invent the electric light bulb.'

Roger Bannister ran the mile in four minutes when all around him believed it couldn't be done.

We don't know if either of these achievers took the best actions to achieve their success, but we do know that they courageously challenged and surpassed the conventional thinking of their time. Their extraordinary thinking has certainly proven more valuable than the condemnation of their critics.

How much of your time is invested in extraordinary thinking?

Are you an extraordinary thinker?

WHAT IS OPTIMAL THINKING?

**Wisdom denotes the pursuit of the best ends
by the best means.**
Francis Hutcheson

Have any of these thoughts ever crossed your mind?

I deserve the best life has to offer.

I am making the most of this situation.

I buy the best.

I deserve to have exactly what I want.

Let's look at the best way to proceed.

What's the best use of my time right now?

I can have it all.

I know exactly what I want and the best way to achieve it.

If you have entertained such thoughts, please welcome yourself into the Optimal Thinking Club.

Peak performers, in my view, are those who employ the most productive action at every given moment. They experience the ultimate level of performance. Many authors and professionals in the personal/professional development field have recently concentrated on the subject of peak performance. They have stated that if you embody such qualities as courage, persistence and self-reliance, and use their suggested techniques and short-cuts for setting goals, managing time and relating to people, then you can be classified as a peak performer.

These qualities and techniques combined with positive thinking are certainly constructive ingredients for success, but what is essential for peak performance is peak or Optimal Thinking. You do not function at your peak when you think in only mediocre or even extraordinary terms.

Optimal Thinking is the real basis of peak performance behaviour. It is the ultimate form of positive thinking and the basis of optimum results. Optimal Thinking is superlative positive thinking. Optimal Thinkers focus on the best or most positive thought at any given time. They take the best actions towards their most important goals and experience peak performance.

When thinking Optimally, you are not concerned with others' concepts of 'the best'. You aren't in competition with anyone. Your interest lies in experiencing the results of your own best thoughts. You are concerned with what 'the best' means to you and attach your own value to it. When considering the purchase of a product, one Optimal Thinker may think the best buy is the top of the range and isn't concerned with price. Another purchaser may consider the best buy to be a bargain at sale time. Needless to say, any time is the best time for some people to go shopping!

Donald Trump, well-known New York businessman, makes many statements of Optimal Thinking in his book *The Art of the Deal.* Take these for example:

All my life I have believed in paying for the best.

I want the best whatever it takes.

Maximise your options.

My philosophy is always to hire the best from the best.

This philosophy has allowed him to achieve triumphs like the following. Six years had passed since Wollman ice-skating rink in New York City had been closed for renovations and thirteen million dollars spent. There was still no progress. The city had dedicated yet another three million dollars to complete the task in eighteen months. Donald Trump undertook the project and completed the renovations in only five months and US$750 000 below the budget. He says he simply found 'the best skating rink builders'.

Many successful companies advertise Optimal standards.

Midas — You midas well have the best
Sharp — Simply the best
Kelloggs — The simple things in life are often the best
Barclays Bank — The best bankers in business
Apple Computer — The power to be your best.™

If you run a business or corporation, you can optimise it with Optimal Thinking. You will need to define its strengths, weaknesses, opportunities, threats, values, objectives and plans by answering Optimal questions like:

What are the greatest strengths of this company?
Who are our best people?
What are our best products/services?
How can we make the most of these strengths?
What are our greatest weaknesses?
What's the best way to minimise them?

Educate everyone in the art of Optimal Thinking. *Optimal Thinkers always focus on the best ways to accomplish the most important goals.*

When the Chief Executive Officer of another prominent company described the primary financial purpose of his company he said, 'To maximise returns to our shareholders'. I knew he was an Optimal Thinker.

Gerry, a football player and Optimal Thinker, was suffering from a knee injury. His doctor told him that he would risk further injury by playing in the grand final, but the decision was his. Gerry asked himself the following Optimal questions: 'What's in my best interest? What's the best solution?'

Leon and Anne, both Optimal Thinkers, had been happily married for twenty years. When asked about the success of their relationship, Leon said, 'Whenever we have an argument, we encourage each other to calm down. We then negotiate the best solution for both of us.' Anne said, 'We both know exactly what we want from the relationship. We always acknowledge each other for doing our best to make the relationship the best it can be.'

Do you think like this? If so, how much of your time is invested in Optimal Thinking?

The exciting aspect of Optimal Thinking is that at this very moment, and at any given time, you can optimise your thoughts. Just as you can choose to think positively or negatively, you can choose to think Optimally or otherwise. *You can easily make the quantum leap!*

Imagine you agree to meet a friend for dinner at an average

restaurant. Your choice of dress is mediocre. Picture your appearance in detail. The restaurant is moderately attractive and the chairs are quite comfortable. The food is somewhat ordinary, nothing to write home about. The background music is OK. Your friend is basically a mediocre thinker. He talks about his work situation for most of the evening. He tells you about an employee who is giving him a hard time. He even cracks some pretty good jokes at the employee's expense. You listen and agree that the person he describes is an imbecile. You don't attempt to find a solution.

Let's tune in on part of the conversation:

MEDIOCRE THINKER: My job is quite good but this guy who works for me has been getting on my nerves lately. He's pretty good at his work but he thinks he should be promoted ahead of someone else who's been there longer. He'd be the first to tell you how great he is at his job, but no-one would be the second. This guy always gives his full 34 per cent!

YOU: This guy sounds like an idiot. Why do you put up with him?

MEDIOCRE THINKER: The director of the company likes him and I don't want to make waves.

YOU: I guess you're just going to have to grin and bear it.

How do you both feel now?

Now imagine yourself as an Optimal Thinker. You arrange to meet the same friend for dinner at your favourite restaurant. You have optimised your appearance for the occasion. The ambience is most attractive and the seating, entirely comfortable. You agree that the food couldn't be better. The resident pianist even plays your favourite music.

Your friend shares his problem. You direct the conversation towards discovering the best solution and the most effective actions to implement it. Just as you do for yourself, you assist him to minimise his weaknesses and maximise his strengths and opportunities. You focus on his best attributes, favourite activities and the best means of achieving his most important goals. You bring out the best in him.

Let's tune in now to some of your Optimal responses to the same comments previously made by your friend:

MEDIOCRE THINKER: My job is quite good but this guy who works for me has been getting on my nerves lately. He's pretty good at his work but he thinks he should be promoted ahead of someone else who's been there longer. He'd be the first to tell you how great he is at his job, but no-one would be the second. This guy always gives his full 34 per cent!

OPTIMAL YOU: It sounds like you're pretty frustrated. What are your alternatives for finding the best solution to this problem?

MEDIOCRE THINKER: Well, I guess I could have a talk with him about the company's policy regarding promotions, or I could send him a memo.

OPTIMAL YOU: What's the best alternative for everyone involved?

MEDIOCRE THINKER: I guess a talk would be better.

OPTIMAL YOU: That sounds good. What's the best way you can approach this talk so that it achieves optimum results?

How do you both feel now? How does it feel to bring out the best in others?

With practice, Optimal Thinking will become second nature to you.

What does Optimal mean to you?

Do you have a pen and notebook handy? If not, take some time to get them now. Recording your insights in writing will help you to get the most out of this Optimal Thinking experience. By completing these Optimal sentences, you will become more acquainted with what Optimal means to you.

My favourite colour is . . .

My most attractive physical feature is . . .

I look my best when . . .

My favourite artist is . . .

The sounds of nature I appreciate most are . . .
My favourite music is . . .
The funniest comedian I have heard is . . .
The singer who has the most pleasing voice is . . .

The most cheerful person I know is . . .
The most comfortable chair in my home is . .
At home, I feel my best when . . .
The most enjoyable vacation I can recall is . . .
The warmest room in my house is . . .

When it comes to friendship my most positive attribute is . . .
What I like most about my best friend is . . .
The greatest skill I bring to my work is . . .
What the best really means to me is . . .
My Optimal fantasy is . . .

By using Optimal questioning techniques you can discover what the best means to you in whichever context you choose. Here is an example:

What do you value most about friendship?
Answer: Trust

What do you value most about trust?
Answer: I can share my innermost thoughts and feelings.

What do you value most about sharing your innermost thoughts and feelings?
Answer: I feel accepted for who I really am.

What do you value most about being accepted for who you really are?
Answer: When I feel accepted, I am more loving.

Continue asking Optimal questions until you are totally satisfied with your response. Then, to evaluate the relative importance of these values, simply look at your list and decide which is most important. When you have identified your highest priority, look through the remaining responses and choose the next most important. Continue until you have defined your priority of values.

The key to the Optimal answer is . . . the Optimal question.

When you ask the best questions of yourself and others, you obtain the best answers. You can even create the Optimal path to your most desired outcomes.

To find the most profitable path to your goal, you simply ask 'most profitable' questions: What's my most profitable activity? How can I optimise the profitability of this activity? What's the most profitable use of my time right now?

You can ask 'most enjoyable' questions to find the most enjoyable path to your goal: What are my most enjoyable activities? How can I maximise my enjoyment of these activities? What's the most enjoyable use of my time right now? What will make this most enjoyable?

Ask 'most efficient' questions to create the most efficient route. What's the most efficient way to handle this? What's the most efficient action I can take?

In an organisation, it's best when everyone thinks in Optimal terms. When one person is off track, then the others can assist by asking the 'best' questions: What's the best way to handle this? What's the best solution? What's the best opportunity we can act upon right now?

Imagine this is the first day of your Optimal life. You are free to design the Optimal alternatives you want. Here are some Optimal questions to ask yourself and others. Perhaps you would like to put them in your own order of priority before answering them.

The Optimal WHAT questions
What do I like/admire most about myself?
What is my greatest asset/talent/ability?
What is my most productive attitude/habit/skill?
What is my most treasured vision of myself?

What do I enjoy most?
What are my favourite activities?
What do I most want to do?
What do I want to have above all else?
What's my most important goal right now?
What's the best action I can take toward it now?
What will make this most pleasurable?

What are the best influences in my life?
What's the best opportunity I can act upon right now?
What's the best solution to my problem/fear?
What's the best use of my time now/next week?

What is my most profitable activity?
What is my greatest interest?
What can I do to make it most profitable?
What's the most cost effective path to my goal?
What's the best price?

What can I do to bring out the best in you?
What are your best suggestions?

The Optimal WHY questions
Why is this my greatest asset?
Why is this my most important goal?
Why is this my best opportunity right now?

Why is this our most profitable product?
Why is this our most popular product?
Why is this the best solution?

The Optimal HOW questions
How can I bring out the best in myself and others?
How can I best utilise my greatest talents and abilities?
How can I most easily attain/maintain peak health and fitness?

How can we make the most of this situation?
How can we be of greatest service to our clients?

How can I reach my goal in the shortest possible time?
How can I most efficiently reach my goal?
How can I reach my goal most pleasurably?
How can I most profitably reach my goal?

The Optimal WHO questions

Who's the most important person in my life?
Who can I count on most?
Who do I admire most?
Who do I most prefer to be with?

Who do I most want to work with?
Who are my best prospects/customers?
Who can I help most?
Who can benefit most from what I have to offer?
Who do I most want to help?
Who's the best person to speak to about this?

The Optimal WHEN questions

When is the best time to take this action?
When's the best time to start this task/project?
When's the best time to complete this project?
When is the best time to talk with you?

The Optimal WHERE questions

Where's your favourite city/beach/ski resort/location?
Where is the best place for us to talk privately?
Where's the best restaurant in this city?
Where will I find the best people?
Where can I most easily relax?
Where is the best place for me to fulfil my most important goals?
Where is my best source of inspiration?

Where's the best location to work?
Where is the best location for most profitable real estate now?

Now write down three Optimal questions to answer for each day of your first Optimal week.

OVERCOMING NEGATIVE CORE BELIEFS

You may be thinking that Optimal Thinking is very simple. I agree. It *is* simple to think in Optimal terms. You have probably employed Optimal Thinking on some or many occasions, but not consistently. Why aren't you continuously employing the thinking which brings you the best of life? Simply because you haven't been shown how. You entered life with the best computer you could wish for — your brain — but forgot to bring an instruction manual. Like most of us, you've been conditioned to desire and expect less than the best. You may have conflicting thoughts about your ability and worthiness to experience your idea of life's greatest offerings. You probably doubt that it's even possible to always enjoy the best life has to offer.

Have you ever asked any of these questions?

Why do some people enjoy the best life has to offer and others don't?

Why do we sabotage our success?

Why do we compromise, accept substitutes and live mediocre lives?

Why are we so committed to our negativity?

You really *do* deserve the best life has to offer. You deserve to experience your concept of the Optimal lifestyle as your reality. Do *you* believe this? Are you ready to discover and overcome the core beliefs that are preventing you from always thinking Optimally?

Some years ago I devised a seminar to discover the most prevalent core beliefs which inhibit and sabotage our success. It was initially designed to uncover, confront and overcome our most damaging mental conditioning. I discovered the following seven major culprits.

1. Something's wrong with me, you or the rest of the world.

**Tolerance is the first principle of community;
it is the spirit which conserves the best that all men think.**
Helen Keller

Although criticism and judgement have been hailed by our society as intelligent applications of an analytical mind, I believe they are entertained mostly by mediocre and negative minds. Unless criticism is employed with the purpose of discovering the best solution to the problem or defect, it is simply another destructive application of negative thinking.

When you are preoccupied with criticism and judgement, you block your expression of anything positive. You enter a negative spiral. Do you attack yourself with statements like, 'I'm not good/smart/rich/attractive enough'? You may judge others with statements like: 'How can you be so stupid?' 'You wear the wrong clothes'. 'You have a strange way of expressing yourself.' If you keep focusing on 'something's wrong with me, you or the rest of the world', that's exactly what you'll experience for the rest of your life. You will sabotage your experiences, friendships and plans by always finding fault with them. When you catch yourself playing 'something's wrong with me, you or the rest of the world', respond to yourself with acceptance and compassion. Then resolve to think as positively as possible about the situation. If something or someone is not serving your best interests, ask, 'What's the best action I can take to overcome or improve this?'

If you adopt the attitude 'I don't want to judge myself/you, I just want to accept/appreciate/give of my best to you' imagine how improved your life will be. We are too busy analysing, criticising and judging ourselves and others, instead of getting on with issues of Optimal importance, issues such as: Why am I here? What's my major objective? What's my most beneficial focus right now? What is the wisest action I can take right now? Who do I most want to share this with?

There are many critics who concentrate on knocking the success of others. These critics carry the virus known as the *Tall Poppy Syndrome*. Don't let critics destroy you. When confronted with a committed critic, respond with a warm, softening statement such as: 'I very much appreciate your interest in me'. Follow up with statements like: 'I'm interested in your most constructive feedback. Would you please share it with me?' or ask: 'Can you give me your most positive thoughts on this?' Tell critics that you prefer to be appreciated rather than criticised. Encourage them to help you make the most of your greatest assets. Ask them to suggest their best alternatives rather than dwell on finding fault with you or your actions. Devise the warmest and most positive responses to their criticism.

A producer watched a video of one of my first television

shows. The interaction with my guests had been enormously inspiring. I had worn what I considered to be an elegant red dress. When asked for his comments, he informed me that I looked like a 'madam' in my red dress. Stunned by his cutting remark, I asked him for his most positive feedback. He quickly rattled off a list of positive remarks. Later he shared with me that our verbal exchange made him realise that it's far more rewarding to acknowledge and make the most of what is good and of value than to criticise. He understood that if you don't appreciate what you have, you may as well not have it.

What do you imagine would happen if you committed yourself to always finding what was *right* with yourself, others and life? You would experience being the right person in the right place at the right time, doing the right thing the right way. Imagine that!

2. I'm not good enough. I don't deserve the best life has to offer. I don't deserve to have what I want.

Only the best is good enough.
Your best is good enough!
Optimal Thinker

Almost all of us would love to travel the world first class, pampered all the way, accommodated in the finest places, chauffeur-driven everywhere in limousines and, of course, never having to pick up a piece of luggage. Do you deserve this? Why do so few of us experience this? Why are so few of us doing whatever is necessary to accumulate the required financial resources?

Many of you don't give yourselves what you really want because you feel unworthy. Whatever you do it's never good enough. As children, you might have been led to believe that your best wasn't good enough. Your parents, teachers and peers may have undermined your confidence because they lacked confidence in themselves. They could have convinced you that you didn't deserve to have what you wanted. You learned to compromise and accept substitutes. Perhaps you still have a problem giving yourself what you really want because of such early experiences. You are setting yourself up to receive what you don't want. You are sabotaging your Optimal lifestyle!

In order to become a consistent Optimal Thinker, you must accept that *you do deserve the best life has to offer.* Are you willing to believe this? Perhaps you already do, but sometimes think in lesser terms when confronted with life's more challenging experiences.

Bill, a science teacher, was promoted to head of the science department. He knew it was the best thing that could have happened to him. When he called his staff together to discuss the syllabus, he felt so nervous that he forgot to take a copy of it to the meeting. He even called several of his staff by the wrong name.

Patricia had always been attracted to Gilbert. When he asked her out to dinner she felt overwhelmed. She worried that her clothes weren't right and whether she was smart enough to hold his attention. The day before the dinner, she came down with the flu.

When Bryan received a top award for his philanthropic activities, he felt tired and depressed. He just didn't feel right about receiving the award.

Until you completely eliminate belief in your lack of worthiness, you will sabotage your plans by creating tiredness, accidents, sickness and other obstacles.

To check where you stand now in relation to the best life has to offer, take a notebook and on the left hand side of the page write repeatedly *I deserve the best life has to offer.* On the right hand side, record the thoughts that come to your mind. You will notice the mediocrity and the conflicting thoughts, feelings and experiences that stop you from experiencing the best in life. Let them pass through, at the same time withdrawing your belief from them. Don't give those old thoughts and past experiences any more power. You may need to answer the question, 'What's the best action I can take to overcome this?' in order to move on to what you want. After a while you will become aware of thoughts and strong feelings about having exactly what you want. You will become energetically connected and committed to the best life can offer you. You will visualise the best means to accomplish your most important goals and your Optimal plans will begin to be activated.

Do you experience or feel that there is not enough of something you need or want? Do you experience shortages: a shortage of money? not enough friends? lack of career prospects? Keep reminding yourself:

I am enough. I do enough. I have enough. There is enough to satisfy me. I am good enough to attract the best life has to offer. I deserve the best life has to offer.

Invest fifteen to twenty minutes each day on this exercise until you are satisfied that you have removed this crippling core belief.

3. I can't have what I want. I can't make it. I don't believe I can.

When you want what you can have,
you can have what you want.
Optimal Thinker

When we believe we can't have what we want, we can become fearful of thinking about what we want because we 'know' we can't have it. How can we eliminate this belief?

Some of you may have been denied what you wanted from an early age. You may have been labelled as selfish for even wanting something for yourself. Do you recall any early experiences which led you to believe you couldn't have what you wanted? As a child Collette was a big thinker. Many people thought she had delusions of grandeur. She was even told that what she wanted didn't exist. Were your aspirations ridiculed? Did you feel uncomfortable sharing your dreams and goals?

In 1980, Collette wrote a list of her most important goals. She was ready to accept that she could have what she wanted. She was willing to stop limiting herself and wanted to free her mind of restrictions. She knew that if she continued to believe she couldn't have what she wanted, that's what would happen.

Whenever she lost track of her goals she repeatedly told herself, 'I can have exactly what I want'. Which Optimal desires are you willing to place your belief in? If you committed yourself to designing your Optimal lifestyle, what would it look like? What's the best action you can take to experience it right now?

During the seminar I mentioned previously, participants

close their eyes and listen to an audio tape. 'I can have exactly what I want', is gently repeated with soothing background music. Many participants experience obstructing thoughts, feelings and visions. Some have recollections of damaging childhood experiences. Some experience no mental chatter and feel extremely inspired and invigorated. Others actually visualise having what they want! Enormous progress is experienced when you eliminate this restricting core belief. If you are strongly committed to the belief that you can't have what you want, you can start by repeating 'I'm willing to believe I can have what I want' or 'I'm willing to have what I want'.

In order to integrate your Optimal thoughts, it is imperative to keep your mind on what you want, and all the reasons why you can have it. Take your mind off what you don't want. Written Optimal affirmations strategically placed in the most appropriate locations will assist you in staying focused. You may like to place your affirmations in your diary or wallet, on the bathroom mirror, refrigerator or dashboard of your car. The best places to display them are where you're most likely to see them. You may be inspired to compose an Optimal poem. If you are a visual person, make your Optimal affirmations as aesthetically pleasing as possible. The best visual representations of your Optimal desires combined with the Optimal question 'What's the best action I can take towards my goal right now?' will keep you steadily on the best track.

If you are predominantly auditory, you can record your Optimal thoughts as lyrics to your favourite tune on a cassette tape. Create your own Optimal song! Listen to it and sing it with fervour as often as possible. Make it your theme song! Sandra, a social worker had always been unproductive during the first hours of the morning. She simply wasn't a morning person. She recorded her affirmations to song on a tape and played it on the way to work. By the time she arrived, she felt terrific. Make a tape and sing yourself into your Optimal state of being. When you come from that state, you will attract more of it around you. You can create your Optimal experience of life. Make it fun!

For those of you who already use affirmations, you can also

record your Optimal desires as statements on an endless cassette. It is best to create pauses between each sentence to enable you to notice your responses. Imagine your Optimal statements recorded with a background of laughter. Perhaps a mixture of background laughter and applause is more to your liking. What do you imagine the effect of this experience would be? You can change your Optimal message whenever you wish.

If you are predominantly feelings oriented, you may wish to claim peace of mind as an Optimal experience. It may be useful to close your eyes and meditate on feeling calm, relaxed and peaceful as you imagine yourself having exactly what you want. You may wish to converse with your intuitive voice in Optimal terms about having what you want.

4. Fear. I can't cope. I can't handle it.

Failure is not trying
Elbert Hubbard

If you knew that you could cope with every possible life situation, would you have anything to fear? The answer to this question is obviously no.

When you optimise your belief in your ability to cope with all situations, you automatically minimise fear. You can do this by empowering yourself continually with statements like: 'I can cope with this!' 'I can handle it!' 'Go for it!' Your security lies not in what you have, but in your knowledge that you can cope with whatever crosses your path.

Three major fears that sabotage your capacity to consistently use Optimal Thinking are fear of failure, fear of rejection and fear of success. The best way to eliminate fear is to *do* whatever you fear. Passing through fear is far better than living with feelings of immobility and helplessness. Are you willing to progress through your greatest fear right now? What's the best action you can take?

Fear of failure. I can't cope with not getting what I want.
All of us have experienced the disappointment of broken dreams. We feel badly when we think of the goals we didn't achieve. Most of us have submitted a proposal which did not gain approval, failed an exam, or evaluated an issue incorrectly.

Do you choose to play it safe rather than risk failing? Do you fear the hurt and disappointment often associated with failure? How much progress can you experience if you allow fear of failure to dominate your thinking?

As a baby, you made numerous attempts to walk before you managed the process successfully. Failure is the educational aspect of progress. Each learning experience arms you with more knowledge to use *next time.*

The following is an inventory of a life history of failures. This man

at age 31 failed in business
at age 32 was defeated in a legislative race
At age 34 failed in business
at age 35 experienced the death of his loved one
at age 36 experienced a nervous breakdown
at age 38 was defeated in an election
at age 43 was defeated in a congressional race
at age 46 was defeated in a congressional race
at age 48 was defeated in a congressional race
at age 55 was defeated in a congressional race
at age 56 failed to become vice-president
at age 58 was defeated in a senatorial race
at age 60 was elected the president of the United States.

He was known as Abraham Lincoln.

Optimal Thinkers confront obstacles and failures by accepting them and taking the best actions to overcome them. They ask: 'What's the best action I can take to overcome this?' or 'What's the best solution?'.

Do you appreciate the value in adversity? Are you aware that adversity shows you what you're made of? It actually inspires internal growth. You need not be concerned with how low you fall. How high you rise above adversity is what counts. A pilot continually corrects his flight course before reaching the chosen destination. He simply notices the deviations and takes the best actions to rectify them.

When faced with obstacles, negative thinkers often give up on their goal. They scold themselves with negative statements like: 'If only I had tried this.' 'Every time I make a little headway, something bad gets in the way.' The price they have to pay seems overwhelming and the rewards do not appear to justify the means. They label their lack of persistence as failure. By concentrating on wrong outcomes, negative thinkers experience fear and program themselves for failure.

You can fuel your motivation to accomplish your goal by constantly reminding yourself of all the benefits you will enjoy once your reach your desired outcome. Visualise your goal as already achieved. Trust in your ability to meet your own needs.

Right now, what would you attempt if you knew there was no chance of failure? Would you act differently? Has fear of failure been holding you back?

Fear of rejection. I can't cope with 'no'.
Many of us did not receive enough nurturing as children. We carry the scars of emotional deprivation throughout our lives. When faced with further rejection from others who are important to us, we are personally affected in direct proportion to our self-esteem.

You may refrain from the pursuit of goals for fear of the scorn, anger or jealousy that you could receive from others. You are afraid of the word 'no'. You want to please others and be acceptable to them. Interestingly, the more rejection you experience, the more knowledge and experience you gain.

It is much easier to approach people you find attractive, make the extra attempt to sell your product, or audition for that part you always wanted, when you view the results (whatever they may be) as a chance to learn, evaluate and grow. The best sales people are those who face the most rejection. By subjecting themselves to many rejections they learn how to handle it. The fear of rejection does not stop them from moving forward.

Many famous actors were rejected on numerous occasions before they became successful. The production studios in Hollywood repeatedly rejected the Australian film *Crocodile Dundee*. They thought it had little box office appeal. Nevertheless, actor Paul Hogan and manager John Cornell persisted. *Crocodile Dundee* was a huge success and broke box office records in the United States.

Eighteen publishers rejected Richard Bach's best-selling

book, *Jonathan Livingstone Seagull.* It was finally published in 1970. By 1975 more than seven million copies had been sold in the U.S., and millions more throughout the world.

Actually there is really no such thing as rejection, only a mismatch of agendas. It is reasonable to expect that people don't always want the same things at exactly the same time. If others don't want you in their lives, don't take it personally. You are just as good as the best of them. Focus on thinking Optimally, feeling as good as possible, doing what feels best, and ask 'Who's next?'

Fear of success. I can't cope with having what I want.
Many of you fear the changes which can accompany success. Perhaps you fear that your success will be gained at someone else's expense or that you may grow away from your spouse in the process. You may fear their disapproval and jealousy. You please others for fear of creating waves.

Recently I spoke with one of the nation's richest men. He told me that he was reluctant to have his name mentioned on any of his company's projects as he did not want to attract the attention of the press. He was convinced that the media would turn on him just as it had done with many of the nation's tall poppies.

Have you suffered as a result of the tall poppy syndrome? Have you limited your progress, for fear of the criticism you may attract? The fears that the tall poppy syndrome instils in individuals and organisations are hindering success on a national and international level. Our education system needs to focus our attention on two vital issues: respect for the individual and respect for success!

In order to associate feelings of safety and comfort with success, record on a cassette tape the following sentences: 'It is safe to be successful. I am comfortable with success. Success belongs to me. Success is my birthright. I was born to succeed. I'm a true success. I enjoy success. I'm optimising my success every minute. I love the benefits of success. I deserve to have it all.' Listen to it over and over again. Repeat these affirmations continually to overcome your fears. Substitute fear with thoughts of safety and enjoyment of success during your daily life.

5. Life is a struggle. It's so hard to go for what I want. It's a jungle out there.

Many of you did not have a very easy home life. You may have had to compete with 'smarter' brothers or sisters and struggled desperately to be their equal in areas which did not utilise your greatest talents. Many a great singer, writer or athlete had to struggle through meaningless maths classes because of compulsory education systems. Your parents may have struggled to make ends meet financially. It may have been a great burden for them to provide the means for you to attend school. You got the message that life is a struggle.

Many people have experienced life as a struggle and truly believe that this is the way it is meant to be. Even the former Prime Minister of Australia, Malcolm Fraser, shared this belief. Some years ago, he declared to the Australian nation that 'Life wasn't meant to be easy!'

We create our own struggles because we continue to entertain thoughts of hardship and struggle. The Optimal antidote for these thoughts is the affirmation, 'I now easily create what I want'.

You can choose goals which are easily attainable and then taking the easiest path towards them by answering questions like: 'What's the easiest way to reach my goal?' 'What's the easiest action I can take?' Once you have achieved some goals without struggling, it will be easier for you to achieve everything you want.

6. I live for today. Today is all that's important. Who knows what will happen tomorrow. I can't plan because I never follow through on my plans.

Research conducted at Harvard University shows that the top 3 per cent of financial achievers in society have written specific goals and plans. They know what they want and how they plan to get there. The next 10 per cent have some goals in mind. The rest have few, if any goals at all. Why do so many avoid setting goals and doing all that is necessary to achieve them?

Most of us were not taught how to set achievable goals or how to go about attaining them. We confront life on a trial-and-error basis day after day, hoping that our desires will be fulfilled.

Many of us set goals in the past which were not achievable and prefer not to set others for fear of further failure.

Do you believe in living exclusively in the present? Is this why you don't plan? Does this really work? It may be enlightening to discover why you adopted this philosophy. You can write down the pros and cons of living exclusively in the present and compare them with the pros and cons of preparing and planning for tomorrow. It is most productive to balance appreciation of the present with planning and achieving your future.

Bear in mind that when you have no goal you simply don't know what you want. Once you have a goal but no plan, you may experience frustration because you don't know how to get what you want. A plan enables you to see how to reach your goal. It provides a blueprint for success. You will experience Optimal success when you take step-by-step action on your Optimal plan.

If you have had trouble planning up till now, reprogram yourself with the following statements: 'I am responsible for the success of my life. I make Optimal plans and follow through on them because I was created to have what I want now, today and tomorrow.'

7. I am not responsible for my life. An outside entity is responsible for my life. Life happens to me.

People are always blaming their circumstances for what they are. I don't believe in circumstances. The people who get on in this world are the people who get up and look for the circumstances they want, and if they can't <u>find them, make them.</u>
George Bernard Shaw

Do you take full responsibility for your life or do you give this responsibility to others? You may not believe in your right to take complete responsibility for creating your path in life. You may experience conflict with your religious beliefs when challenged to take full responsibility for your life's direction. You may be convinced that people are here to follow divine direction. When you are guided by your religious beliefs, are they sufficient to help you achieve all you want? Do you need to take more control of your life? Do you accept what is out of your control and optimise what you can control?

Perhaps you were brought up to believe that your role in life is to support others and that your personal goals and desires are secondary. You feel selfish when you consider yourself first. You make your happiness dependent on others and offer them the opportunity to make or break you. Many a divorcee has rebelled against this type of early conditioning.

Some people see themselves as victims of life. They believe that life happens to them. If it hadn't been for this, that or the other, they would be doing very well now. Blame is often the name of the victim's game. Whenever you're angry with someone, ask yourself 'What am I not doing for myself that I am blaming others for not doing for me?' Once you realise what it is you're not doing for yourself, you can take the best corrective actions.

John, an engineer, felt stuck in a job he absolutely detested. He talked continually about changing his career yet did nothing about it. He was convinced that he was a victim of circumstance. How could he possibly change careers at forty-seven years of age? Employers were interested in young blood. It was too late. If only he had done something about it when he was younger. By assuming the victim role, John did not have to face the risk of rejection in a new career search. He could continue to put in a thirty-hour-week and enjoy a game of tennis after work every night. Even though he hated his work, he earned a fine salary, was respected by management and his peers and could arrange his working hours as he wished.

When John evaluated the benefits of his present job and stopped playing the victim, he took control of his life. He decided to invest six hours every week investigating job possibilities. Within four months he found a new job he now thoroughly enjoys. He stopped being a victim and chose to become a victor.

You can convert negative victim thinking into Optimal victor thinking by placing your belief in the following statement. 'I take full responsibility for optimising my thoughts, actions, feelings and life.'

OPTIMAL AFFIRMATIONS

*I am an Optimal Thinker.
I focus on the most positive
thought at every given
moment.*

▼

*I now resolve to get the most
out of this book.*

▼

*I deserve to have exactly
what I want.*

▼

*I deserve the best life has
to offer.*

▼

*I can have exactly what
I want.*

▼

*I always create what I need
and want.*

▼

*I am now enjoying the best
life has to offer.*

I give myself what I really want and feel I deserve it.

▼

I focus on what I want and all the reasons I can have it.

▼

I'm the best person in the best place concentrating on the best activity in the best way.

▼

I expect only the best to happen and it does!

▼

I have everything I need to have everything I want.

▼

I choose the highest, first!

▼

All my needs are met.

▼

I can have it all.

MONITOR YOURSELF AS AN OPTIMAL THINKER

Optimal Thinkers choose to see themselves as the best person, in the best place, at the best time, engaged in the best activity in the best way.

To monitor your effectiveness as an Optimal Thinker, ask yourself: 'What percentage of today was I the right or best person in the best place involved in the best activity in the best way? How much of this week? What percentage of this month?

James, an extraordinary thinker and real estate salesman, felt very pleased with his progress. He was doing very well at work. He had recently moved into a new home which was almost ideally suited to his needs. He had lots of fine friends and hobbies and always had something interesting to do. He evaluated his effectiveness as an Optimal Thinker as follows:

	Percentage of Day as Optimal Thinker	Percentage of Week as Optimal Thinker
best person	90	90
best place	90	90
best time	90	80
best activity	85	90
best way	85	75

James became more aware of his thinking, and as a result, committed himself to continually optimising his thoughts. He engaged a top interior decorator to help him furnish his home in the best possible way. He used the extra time to maximise his skills at work.

Lionel, a mediocre thinker, was reasonably happy with his life but things could have been better. He would have liked to live in a nicer home but didn't have the means. He had a secure but unstimulating job. He evaluated his effectiveness as an Optimal Thinker as follows:

	Percentage of Day as Optimal Thinker	Percentage of Week as Optimal Thinker
best person	65	65
best place	55	60
best time	60	60
best activity	40	40
best way	65	65

Lionel thought that he could do better than this and decided to find a stimulating job that paid more. In time he would be able to afford the home he really wanted.

Ellen, a secretary and negative thinker, felt trapped. She didn't like city living in general, but wasn't sure where she wanted to be. She resented having to work, didn't like her job and complained constantly. Ellen evaluated her effectiveness as an Optimal Thinker like this:

	Percentage of Day as Optimal Thinker	Percentage of Week as Optimal Thinker
best person	25	25
best place	5	5
best time	0	0
best activity	0	0
best way	25	25

Ellen realised that negative thinking was stopping her from enjoying life. She recorded some Optimal affirmations on a cassette tape and listened to them every morning. She even decided to make the most of her job while she was deciding where she wanted to be.

You should start monitoring your progress right now. Simply answer the same questions about how you use your time. Schedule the best time to do this on a regular basis.

When you use Optimal Thinking consistently you will enjoy the best life has to offer!

CHAPTER TWO

UNDERSTANDING YOURSELF TO CREATE YOUR OPTIMAL PROFILE

I deserve the best in life.
Optimal Thinker

SELF-ESTEEM: WHAT'S IT ALL ABOUT?

'I have trouble forming a healthy intimate relationship with a man because deep down I don't feel good enough.'

'When everything is going right, this little voice inside me says this is too good to be true, and sure enough, something goes wrong. I can't seem to win!'

'I feel guilty whenever I argue with anyone, even when I know I'm right.'

It all started when you were growing up. Your parents and other important people gave you many signals about the kind of person you were. Some of their signals were encouraging, loving and validating. They may have said: 'I love you.' 'You are my pride and joy.' 'You're a clever girl.' 'You can succeed at anything when you put your mind to it.' Other messages from these authorities were far from Optimal and certainly not affirmative. You may have been subjected to statements like: 'What did you do a dumb thing like that for?' 'You never do anything right.' 'You're a bad boy.'

What you thought about yourself, and how you felt when receiving those messages, formed the basis of your self-esteem. Your level of self-esteem today is based on the thoughts and feelings you have accumulated about yourself since that time.

The way you think and feel about yourself affects every aspect of your life. When you love, accept, respect and approve of yourself, you validate your existence. Do you feel worthy of life's best offerings? Do you feel confident that you can experience the best in life? Do you respect yourself? Would you like to experience Optimal self-esteem?

Perhaps you dislike yourself. People with low self-esteem feel there is something wrong with them. They are extremely self-critical and feel badly about themselves. They lack self-confidence and self-respect. They consider themselves incompetent and unworthy of the best things in life. Do you identify with this description? Is so, are you willing to learn how to minimise those thoughts and feelings?

Many people experience great success yet feel empty inside. Some are admired by their spouses, business associates and friends but feel unworthy. Others are honoured with awards for their actions yet deep down regard themselves as incompetent.

Marilyn Monroe, superstar actress, was such a person. Even though she was crowned as a sensational beauty, adored by the masses, and pursued by the most powerful men of her day, Marilyn felt so bad about herself that she chose to end her life.

Perhaps you fluctuate between liking and disliking yourself? People with average self-esteem fluctuate between feeling good and bad, right and wrong, and worthy and undeserving. At times they are confident and at other times uncertain. Does this describe you?

OUR INTERNAL VOICES

Self-esteem entails a sense of personal confidence and worthiness. It is an internal experience. When we are compassionate toward our weaknesses and forgive ourselves for making mistakes, we accept the reality of our humanness. When we validate ourselves and trust our internal voices, we esteem ourselves. We all experience internal chit-chat. Represented below are some inner voices. Which do you identify with most?

Optimal voice — your most positive voice!

Is interested in the most positive, everything superlative, the best, mastery, completion, supremacy; the impeccable, peak, top, maximum, optimum, uppermost, ultimate, highest, largest, paramount, paragon, Optimal!

It Optimises, maximises, masters, epitomises, perfects, corrects, solves, completes, fulfils, fills, wins, triumphs, accomplishes, succeeds, heads, accepts, appreciates, leads.

Listen to these Optimal voices:

I accept myself warts and all. I deserve the best life has to offer.

I am doing the best I can!

I'm making the most of my situation.

I have completed every project on budget and on time for the last seven years.

To make the best use of your Optimal voice, start by affirming your right to be exactly as you are without justification or judgement. Accept, approve and love yourself unconditionally. *You are doing your best according to your awareness at this time!*

Other Voices
Negative voice
Is interested in criticism, judgement, attack, slander, harm, hurt, disadvantage, frustration, failure, fault-finding, destruction, tragedy, inferiority, weakness, loss, injury, aggravation.

It criticises, demeans, slanders, blames, sabotages, undermines, depreciates, hurts, rejects, disapproves, doubts, worries, fears, discourages, condemns, weakens.

Positive voice
Is interested in the certain, beneficial, sound, confident, assured, unquestionable, constructive, affirmative, accepted, valuable.

It assures, encourages, inspires, validates, empowers, affirms, confirms, supports, uplifts, respects, appreciates, esteems, enjoys, strengthens.

Ineffective voice
Is interested in the fruitless, inefficient, incapable, incompetent, unqualified, unproductive, inadequate, unsatisfactory, incon-sequential, worthless, useless, inappropriate, insufficient.

It invalidates, flounders, impedes, fails, has no effect.

Effective voice
Is interested in the competent, capable, able, qualified, satisfactory, proficient, accurate.

It qualifies, accepts, achieves, actualises, secures, produces, creates, generates, succeeds, implements.

Mediocre voice
Is interested in the ordinary, fair, good, common, commonplace, average, insignificant, customary, usual, conventional, run of the mill, unnoticeable, moderate.

It compromises, averages, takes the middle path.

Extraordinary voice

Is interested in the great, outstanding, remarkable, exceptional, stunning, sensational, astounding, fabulous, phenomenal, incredible, mammoth, uncommon, unusual.

It surpasses, exceeds, stands out, stuns, distinguishes, impresses.

Optimising your Other Voices

Do your Other Voices talk too much? Are you ready to minimise their influence? Conquering your negative voice is a necessary requirement for a healthy self-concept. Optimising your Other Voices is your commitment to your highest level of self-esteem.

You can optimise your internal talk by using your Optimal voice at every opportune moment. When your Other Voices chatter, commission *Optimax*, your best self, friend, imaginary mentor or favourite comedian, to talk back to them. Optimax is an Optimal Thinker and always emphasises the best in you. Optimax always outwits and triumphs over your Other Voices.

Let's tune in on Optimax's reactions to your negative and ineffective voices.

NEGATIVE VOICE: I feel like a real loser.

OPTIMAX: I hear what you say. What's the best action you can take to feel successful right now?

NEGATIVE VOICE: I should have eaten less. It's very difficult to get rid of this extra weight!

OPTIMAX: I know you're feeling guilty and overweight. What's the best thing you could do right now to stop feeling guilty and start losing weight?

INEFFECTIVE VOICE: I feel incompetent. I'm trying hard and not getting results.

OPTIMAX: You're feeling ineffective. What's the best way to achieve the results you want? What's the best use of your time?

To optimise your Other Voices, it is best to start by writing your responses on paper. Carry a notebook around with you. Jot down the message from your Other Voices, then write Optimax's rebuttals. When the technique becomes second nature, you can do it mentally.

Now let's listen to Optimax triumph over your Other Voices.

EFFECTIVE VOICE: I produced a fine video. I'm pleased with it.

OPTIMAX: I'm pleased for you. What did you like most about it?

MEDIOCRE VOICE: Some pretty good opportunities come my way from time to time.

OPTIMAX: That's interesting. What's the best opportunity you can act upon right now?

MEDIOCRE VOICE: I'm pretty good at resolving conflicts.

OPTIMAX: That's good. What's the most important thing about resolving conflict that you can keep in mind to optimise your skills?

EXTRAORDINARY VOICE: I feel terrific right now.

OPTIMAX: I'm happy to hear that. How can you make the most of it?

EXTRAORDINARY VOICE: My business is flourishing.

OPTIMAX: I'm glad to hear that. What is your most profitable product? How can you optimise its profitability?

HOW DO YOU VALUE AND RATE YOURSELF NOW?

Your assets

Many people feel uncomfortable talking openly about their strengths. When they were growing up, their parents and teachers cautioned them against boasting. They were criticised for being braggarts when they talked highly about themselves. 'Actions speak louder than words' was a statement many of us heard repeatedly. Do you recall conversations like these?

YOU: I did really well in the maths test, Mum. I got an A!

MUM: When you get an A+ you can say you did really well. Until then, you'd better buckle up and improve the standard of your work.

YOU: I rode my bike all the way to the shops, Dad.

DAD: Don't do that again. It's very dangerous.

It is now time to do some personal stocktaking. Make sure you are in a quiet place where you won't be disturbed. You will need your pen and notebook. Be diligent in following the written instructions.

The seven categories below have been chosen to assist you in describing your assets accurately. For each category write down your positive attributes. Note what you like about yourself. Be as specific as possible. After you have identified your strengths, arrange them in order of greatest benefit to you. On the top of your asset inventory, list your greatest asset and then proceed down your list with those assets which are of lesser benefit to you.

Anne, a successful public relations executive, invested half an hour defining her hierarchy of assets with the following list.

1. Bodily assets
Large blue eyes
Well shaped mouth, white teeth
Long blonde hair
Well shaped calves
Well proportioned body
Good height 162 cm (5 ft 4 in)
Look good in fitted clothing

2. Mental strengths
Intuitive
Mostly positive, sometimes Optimal
Single-minded when necessary
Good knowledge of world affairs
Polished with spontaneous humour
Confident about intellectual capability
Logical
Creative thinker

3. Personality strengths
Inspiring
Extrovert
Open
Talkative
Responsible
Warm
Fun
Fairly even tempered

4. Social strengths
Sincere
Communicate openly
Interested in others
Warm, caring
Generally positive
Good listener, compassionate
Entertaining
Confident

5. Career and/or daily task strengths
Generally keep word
Competent P.R. skills
Excellent face-to-face presentation skills
Punctual
Well-organised
Establish good rapport with clients

6. Sexual strengths
Enjoy sex only with loving partner
Can initiate
Sensual
Enjoy pleasing partner
Can discuss sexual preferences verbally

7. Personal achievements
Top P.R. person in company this year
Offered a 20 per cent salary increase
Key speaker at P.R. Institute convention
Bought three bedroom home
Lost over 13 kg (30 lb) last year
Established supportive group of friends

8. What I like most about myself. What makes me feel best about myself. What makes me feel competent and worthwhile.

I am tenacious
I have a good sense of humour
Can be very positive and inspiring
Attractive appearance
Warm, kind and caring to family, friends and others

Your liabilities

Now, for each category, write a list of your negative traits. When addressing your weaknesses and limitations, it is important to avoid the use of disparaging terminology. Be specific and non-judgemental. For example, instead of saying 'I have terrible skin', say 'At the moment there are two blemishes on my cheeks'. Instead of 'I'm a fat slob', substitute 'I'm 6 kg (15 lb) overweight'. After you have identified your weaknesses, define them in order of priority. On the top of your liability inventory, note your greatest liability and then proceed down your list with those liabilities which are less of a problem to you.

Anne's liability inventory took the following form.

1. Bodily liabilities

Wrinkles around eyes
Nearly 3 kg (6 lb) overweight
Thighs 2.5–5 cm (1–2 in) too large
Cellulite on upper legs
Freckles, liver spots and scars on skin
Poor muscle tone

2. Mental liabilities

Repeat self on occasion, repeat self on occasion, repeat self . . .
Overly critical
Too negative
Perfectionist

3. Personality weaknesses
Dogmatic on occasion
Argumentative at times
Overly talkative
Moody
Compromise integrity on unimportant issues

4. Social weaknesses
Overly critical of others
Can be loud
Fluctuate in feelings toward people
Can be unforgiving
Easily upset by others' put-downs

5. Career and/or daily task weaknesses
Wavering dedication and motivation
Inconsistent
Poor delegation skills

6. Sexual weaknesses
Feel hurt when rejected

7. What I dislike most about myself. What makes me feel bad about myself. What makes me feel incompetent and unworthy.
I am overly critical of myself and others
My two marriages were disasters and I don't have a suitable boyfriend now
I feel like a failure when I am around couples with children
I am overweight
My body is not sufficiently toned
I can't cook

When Anne completed her list of weaknesses she noticed the items mentioned were more specific than those on her strengths inventory. She realised that she had always focused more attention on her liabilities than her assets.

Your self-esteem
How would you describe your self-esteem? Do you have low, average, high or Optimal self-esteem? Take some time now to

jot down your thoughts and feelings about yourself. When Anne wrote how she felt about herself in the paragraph below, she realised she wavered in her liking for herself.

Sometimes I like myself and feel good. At other times, I dislike myself and feel inadequate. I guess I have average self-esteem. I seem to have extraordinarily high self-esteem when it comes to my work and social life. In other areas there is lots of room for improvement. At times I feel like a failure because I haven't managed to find a life partner and have a family. I also hate myself when I compromise my principles over silly issues. I don't know why I do that.

YOUR OPTIMAL PROFILE

It is time to embrace your Optimal profile. This is the profile of yourself that encourages your highest level of self-esteem. It inspires your ultimate experience of self-confidence and self-respect and urges you to see yourself as a total winner.

Below are some Optimal techniques, suggestions and questions to help you make your profile completely concrete.

Optimising your assets

Take out the notebook in which you listed your assets and liabilities and look at your list of assets. Now, under each asset, write the best actions you can take to appreciate, optimise and enjoy the full benefit of it. *It is best to accept what you can't change and optimise what you can!* You may think, 'It would be terrific to be taller!' In this case, all you can do is accept your height, focus on all the advantages of being as tall as you are and make the most of it.

To optimise an asset, you can ask the Optimal question:

How can I make the most of this asset?

Appreciate all your assets by reminding yourself of all the benefits you enjoy because of them. You can do this at every opportune moment.

The list opposite represents a selection of Anne's contribution.

1. Bodily assets

Large blue eyes

Optimise by appreciating this asset daily; investigate best makeup to optimise size, colour and shape of eyes.

2. Mental assets

Intuitive

Optimise by appreciating this asset daily; make sure to trust and follow my intuition at every opportune moment.

Mostly positive, sometimes Optimal

Optimise by appreciating this asset daily; place Optimal signs in strategic places to remind me to think Optimally.

3. Personality strengths

Inspiring

Optimise by appreciating this asset daily; encourage Ray to finish his project.

Extrovert

Optimise by appreciating this asset daily.

4. Social strengths

Communicate openly

Optimise by appreciating this asset daily; tell my friends that I wish to support their best endeavours and ask them to share with me how I can best do this.

Interested in others

Optimise by appreciating this asset daily; ask others about their greatest pleasures. Find out what I can do to bring out the best in them.

5. Career and/or daily task strengths

Excellent face to face presentation skills

Optimise by appreciating this asset daily; schedule one hour each day to optimise presentations.

6. Sexual strengths

Can initiate

Optimise by appreciating this asset daily.

7. Personal achievements

Offered a 20 per cent salary increase

Optimise by appreciating this asset daily; book a holiday to Hawaii; buy a new dining room suite.

Established supportive group of friends

Optimise by appreciating this asset daily; make sure I speak to each of them at least once a week. Invite friends over at least once every fortnight.

8. What I like most about myself. What makes me feel best about myself. What makes me feel competent and worthwhile.

Can be very positive and inspiring

Optimise by appreciating this asset daily; affirm: 'I am an Optimal Thinker. I am now optimising my mental attractiveness. I am the most inspiring person I can possibly be'.

When Anne wrote her list of actions to optimise her assets, she identified, in order or priority, the actions which would have the most positive effect on her self-confidence and self-respect. Enthusiastically, she took the actions necessary to experience herself at her best. What did you discover when you wrote out your inventory of personal assets and the best actions to optimise them? Did you give yourself reasonable time frames to complete your Optimal actions? It is best to transfer your list to your daily calendar to ensure that they get done. Allow me to encourage you to DO IT NOW!

Minimising your liabilities

To minimise any weakness, simply answer the following Optimal questions:

What are all the benefits I will gain by correcting this weakness?
What's the best way to minimise this weakness?
What's the best action I can take NOW to move toward what I want?

Jim was an athlete but an injury had forced him to stop his sporting activities. He had joined the gym but attended only sporadically. Jim's body had deteriorated. He was not as muscular as he would have liked. He felt badly about his body but could rarely motivate himself to lift weights or exercise. He answered the Optimal questions as follows:

What are all the benefits I will gain by correcting this weakness?
Strength and power, more self-confidence, pride in myself, feel more attractive to women, at my best.

What's the best way to minimise this weakness?
Carry photo of myself with muscular body in wallet to remind myself how great I can look and feel. Schedule an hour, five mornings a week, from 6:30–7:30 am, to work out at gym. When I'm working out, stay focused on the end result — the muscular body that makes me feel best about myself. Every time I work out, reward myself by taking an extra half hour to do something I really enjoy.

What's the best action I can take NOW to move toward what I want?
Put photo in wallet. Prepare my workout gear for tomorrow morning.

Now, go through your list of weaknesses and decide to accept yourself unconditionally. Resolve to correct the weaknesses which can be changed. Write down the best actions you can take to minimise your liabilities and negative traits.

Anne felt terrific when she completed her list. Here is a selection.

1. Bodily liabilities
Poor muscle tone

Minimise by accepting this; investigate most suitable ways of optimising muscle tone; call local Yoga teacher and ask for schedule.

2. Mental liabilities
Repeat self on occasion, repeat self on occasion, repeat self . . .

Minimise by accepting this; be more aware of it and stop whenever I notice myself doing it.

Overly critical

Minimise by accepting this; affirm: 'I now focus on what's right with myself and others. I am an Optimal Thinker. Whenever I briefly focus on a problem it's only because I'm looking for the best solution'.

3. Personality weaknesses

Argumentative at times

Minimise by accepting this; ask: 'Is this the best thing to do right now? Can I be more productive in this situation by not arguing?'

Overly talkative

Minimise by accepting this; ask: 'What's the best use of my time right now?' Be aware of the time I waste by talking too much.

4. Social weaknesses

Can be loud

Minimise by accepting this; make a concerted effort to speak softly.

Easily upset by others' put-downs

Minimise by accepting this; get back on track by affirming: 'This will pass. What's the best action I can take to overcome this?' or 'I am now choosing to focus on what makes me feel best about myself'.

5. Career and/or daily task weaknesses

Wavering dedication and motivation

Minimise by accepting this; schedule time on Monday to clarify the purpose of my work and its priority in my life.

6. Sexual weaknesses

Feel hurt when rejected

Minimise by accepting each rejection as a chance to learn and grow.

7. What I dislike most about myself. What makes me feel bad about myself. What makes me feel incompetent and unworthy.

I am overly critical of myself and others.

Minimise by accepting this; affirm: 'I now focus on what's right with myself and others. I only criticise when I am interested in finding the best solution to the problem'.

I can't cook.

Minimise by accepting this; start using every opportune moment in the kitchen to optimise my cooking skills. Take cooking lessons.

When Anne completed her list of actions to correct her weaknesses, she noticed again that they were more specific than those on her strengths inventory. She had always been interested in self-improvement. She realised that she had formed the habit of finding fault with herself, and correcting her flaws to temporarily avoid feeling badly about herself. By neglecting to appreciate and optimise her strengths, she had robbed herself of self-esteem. She determined the priority of her most important actions by asking:

Which action will be most beneficial to my self-confidence and self-respect?

In this way, from her lists, she was able to choose the best actions to raise her self-esteem most effectively. When she finished optimising her assets, she concentrated on minimising her weaknesses.

Look at your list of liabilities, then write down in order of priority, the actions you will take to minimise your weaknesses. Be sure to allow reasonable time and to place your prioritised list in your daily calendar.

Use Optimal affirmations at every opportune moment

Optimal affirmations are first person, present tense, Optimal statements which you immerse in your mind to produce Optimal results. They are verbal 'act as if . . .' statements. Here are some Optimal affirmations you may wish to adopt.

Optimal affirmations for body

I enjoy Optimal health. It's my birthright.
I accept my body completely. I am making the most of it.
Everything I eat produces my Optimal health, beauty and weight.
My body is in Optimal condition.
I am looking my best.
I am now enjoying my Optimal physical attractiveness.

Optimal affirmations for mind

I am an Optimal Thinker. I focus on the most positive thought at every given moment.
I now resolve to be the best I can be.
I am doing my best.
My best investment is in the best.
I am now enjoying the best life has to offer.
I can have exactly what I want.
I make the most of my mind.

Optimal social affirmations

I attract the right people.
I bring out the best in others.
I have all the friends I need.
I ask for what I want.
My behaviour is always appropriate.
I choose to accept and love others as they are.

Once you have decided which Optimal affirmations you wish to integrate, you can create visual reminders, or write them repeatedly in your notebook and note your responses. You can also meditate on them, sing them, or record them on a cassette tape and listen to them whenever you want.

Recall your successes

Optimal Thinkers constantly remind themselves of their past successes. They can recall countless occasions when they achieved exactly what they wanted.

Do you take your success for granted? David, an entrepreneur, keeps a victory journal. Every time he gets what he wants he writes down his successful experience. Whenever he doubts himself or faces a frightening experience he goes to his victory journal for inspiration. He immediately regains access to his Optimal state. Do you acknowledge your successes often enough? Do you see yourself as a success?

Visualise your Optimal profile
Visualise yourself at your best

Our minds can't distinguish between what we visualise and what we actually experience. There have been many experiments performed which support this. One well-known experiment by psychologists involved a number of men who were divided into three groups. One group practised basketball on the court every day, the second mentally visualised themselves practising and the third control group did neither. The study found that the men who physically practised and those who mentally practised were equally good on the court. The control group was severely beaten by both other groups.

Other experiments have shown that when people visualise themselves performing an action, running for example, the muscles associated with that action contract in small but definite amounts. You can prove this to yourself by closing your eyes and imagining yourself sucking on a lemon. Your mouth will pucker and start to water.

Optimal visualisation enables you to convey exactly what you want to your subconscious by using the best pictures and symbols and all of your senses. By giving yourself the Optimal preview of your desired result it becomes real and concrete and you prepare yourself to experience the best. You start to adjust yourself toward having what you want by incorporating it physically, emotionally and mentally. Optimal visualisation hastens the process of reaching your most desired goals.

You can easily visualise yourself at your best. Here is an example of visualisation to help you clarify your Optimal profile.

Find a comfortable environment where you will not be disturbed. Close your eyes and take a few deep breaths. Take it easy. Relax . . .

Picture yourself involved in an activity where you feel completely in control. You may wish to direct your attention toward the simple process of breathing. Relax into the feeling of total mastery. Think about everything in your life that encourages you to feel completely competent and confident.

Now see yourself accepting your body completely. Focus your appreciation on the blessings you experience by living in your body. Reflect on what you like most about your body. Imagine your body at its best. See it and experience in detail. You deserve to have the body you want.

Now imagine your Optimal mind set. Focus your attention on your most positive thoughts. Listen to your Optimal voice. Allow Optimax to share its Optimal viewpoints with you. Imagine an Optimal conversation with whoever you want.

Imagine your personality at its best. Take some time to appreciate and enjoy it. What do you see, what can you hear and how do you feel?

Now experience your Optimal social self. Surround yourself with your favourite people who accept you as you are and delight in your best efforts. See yourself at your best bringing out the best in others. Imagine demonstrating your best social skills.

Now see yourself at your peak in your career. You are doing your best. You love what you do and are appropriately rewarded for your efforts. You are making the ultimate use of every moment. You are achieving exactly what you want.

Now see and experience your Optimal sexual self. Take enough time to imagine experiencing exactly what you want.

Focus now on your greatest accomplishment. You can project as far into the future as you want. Enjoy your greatest victory. Experience every aspect of it. See yourself as a total winner. You do deserve the best life has to offer!

Record your vision of your Optimal profile in your notebook right now.

COMMITTING YOURSELF TO YOUR OPTIMAL PROFILE

Below are some Optimal questions which will assist you to commit wholeheartedly to making your Optimal profile your reality.

What are all the benefits I will experience by realising my Optimal profile?

To fuel your motivation to embrace your Optimal profile, jot down all the benefits you will gain by embodying the profile. Keep your list with you.

How will I think and feel by realising my Optimal profile?

Imagine your thoughts and feelings when you totally accept yourself and experience yourself at your best. Consider especially what Optimal self-confidence and self-respect feel like. Hold on to your vision. There is no need to wait for this experience. You can begin it now.

If this is what I want, why don't I have it already?

Now write down any possible obstacles that are in the way of your real life experience of your Optimal profile.

OPTIMAL AFFIRMATIONS

I accept myself completely.

▼

I am wise, I optimise!

▼

I now resolve to be the best I can be!

▼

I am doing my best.

▼

I can't do better than my best!

▼

I am committed to being the best I can be.

▼

Right now, I am the best I can be.

▼

I know, see, hear, feel and experience the best life has to offer me.

▼

I am now making the most of my greatest assets.

What are the best actions I can take to overcome these obstacles?

Identify and note the best solutions to overcome all obstacles. Determine their priority and move into action.

Place your description of your Optimal profile in an Optimal location and read it every day. You can also listen to an endless cassette tape describing the profile. Looking into the mirror and talking to yourself in Optimal terms at least once a day will definitely hasten the optimising process. Remind yourself of your greatest assets and every possible reason for liking and loving yourself. When you concentrate your best efforts on achieving your Optimal profile, you will experience your Optimal state.

CHAPTER THREE

COMMITTING TO YOUR OPTIMAL PURPOSE

I am now committing my best efforts to achieving my Optimal purpose.
Optimal Thinker

IDENTIFYING YOUR OPTIMAL PURPOSE

For the past six years Stephen, a successful businessman, has been living with a woman he doesn't love. He can't summon the courage to end the relationship. Stephen drinks heavily at night. 'It's better than the feeling of emptiness I experience when I'm sober,' he rationalises.

Rhonda enjoyed her role as a devoted mother. Since her two children moved out of home she feels a big gap in her life. She tries to keep herself busy. Rhonda has many friends and is invited to numerous social events. 'What am I doing here? Why am I here?' she asks herself. Most of the time she feels out of place.

John, a computer consultant, often feels tired and depressed. It is difficult for him to get out of bed in the morning. He is plagued with thoughts like: 'Everything feels meaningless. I don't have a reason to live any more. I don't have a purpose.'

Much has been written about the necessity of a meaningful purpose in life. Many of us, however, are unsure of our purpose. At times we know what we want and at other times our souls cry out for direction. Some search for a solution to their emptiness by trying to answer questions like: 'What's it all about? Why am I here? What do I want to do with my life?' Others do whatever they can to avoid their painful thoughts and feelings.

Your Optimal purpose defines your Optimal direction in life. It is your most important reason for being. Your statement of purpose does not need to be specific or measurable. Your goals provide the specific, measurable and reachable steps you will require to fulfil your Optimal purpose.

Do you relate to any of the following statements of purpose?

To be a happy and positive person
To love and be loved
To enjoy health, happiness and prosperity
To be financially independent
To provide a comfortable lifestyle for my family
To be a student of life
To be the best I can be
To make full use of my positive thinking potential.

Optimal Thinkers are devoted to the fulfilment of their Optimal purpose. They know what they are most committed to, what they stand for above all else, and what they most want to achieve.

Jack was happily married and loved his thirteen-year-old son very much. He enjoyed the benefits of family life while accepting its limitations. He wanted to provide the best things in life for his family and worked hard to make a fine living. Since he had entered the video production business, he had often lied to gain new accounts. He felt badly about his lack of integrity. He hated having to lie to make a living.

The following questions assisted Jack and will help you to identify your Optimal purpose. Make sure you have some quiet time and your pen and notebook with you. Note Jack's responses to the questions below and then write down your own. When you have many responses to a particular question, jot them all down. Then decide which one is most important to you.

1. What do I care about most deeply? What and who do I love?
Being a decent person — acting out of integrity
My family
Friends — Jim, Mary, Adrian, Steven, Sandra
Doing work I enjoy and am good at
Feeling happy

Which one is most important to me?
My family

2. What am I deeply committed to?
My family
Being a decent person — acting out of integrity
Doing work I enjoy

Which one is most important to me?
My family

3. What do I stand for?
Honesty
Positivity
Being a decent person — acting out of integrity
Sensitivity
Non-violence
Kindness

Which one is most important to me?
Being a decent person — acting out of integrity

4. When am I at my best?
When I am playing golf with my son
When I relax with my family
When I am producing videos for my favourite clients
When I am happy
When I don't have any financial problems
When I am thinking Optimally

Which one is most important to me?
Thinking Optimally

5. What has given me the greatest feelings of importance in my life? What has enhanced my self-esteem most?
Seeing the effects of my presence on my son
Being a good family man
Going into business for myself

Which one is most important to me?
Being a good family man

6. What is it that I definitely don't want?
(Defining what you don't want is an excellent intermediate step when you don't feel emotionally connected to a purpose. Once you know what you definitely don't want, then the opposite generally reveals what you definitely do want.)

To let my family down
To be poverty stricken
To be unsuccessful in business
To be confused about what I want
To be negative and feel badly about myself, my family and life

To feel guilty
To feel like a phony
To feel that my life is not worthwhile
To be around people I don't admire
To be miserable
To have no integrity
To be intolerant and impatient
To be without friends

Which one is the worst for me?
To feel that my life is not worthwhile

7. What do I want more than anything else?

Be a good family person
Be financially comfortable
Be very successful in business
Be clear about what I want
Be thinking as positively as possible about myself, my family and life
Be full of love, to love life
Be honest about myself
To feel my life is worthwhile
To admire the people around me
Be happy — to spend as much time as possible doing what I enjoy
To keep my integrity intact
Be patient and tolerant
Have friends I care for
Send my son to university
Have enough money to be able to do what I want whenever I want

Which one is most important to me?
To feel my life is worthwhile

8. Which activities do I enjoy most?

Being with my family
Dancing
Reading
Going to the movies
Walking along the beach

Being with friends
Playing golf
Spending money on feeling great
Attending seminars on personal development
Listening to tapes of inspirational speakers
Finalising large transactions
Fine dining

Which one is most important to me?
Being with my family

9. In order of priority, what are the three things I value most in life?

My family
Being a decent person — acting out of integrity
To think as positively as possible about myself, my family and life

10. In order of priority, what are my three most important ambitions in life?

For my family and me to be happy
Keep my integrity intact
Think as positively as possible about myself, my family and life

11. If I had one year to live, how would I make the most of it?

Spend a lot more time in my holiday house
Invest in the best life insurance coverage so that my family will be well taken care of
List in priority all the activities I enjoy and do them
Definitely spend as much time as possible with my family

12. If I were given all the money I could ever need or want, how would I live my life?

Spend much more time with my family
Concentrate on the activities I enjoy most

13. If I could experience the Optimal day, what would it be like?

(How would you start the best day of your life? Where would you most want to be? What would you do? Who would you choose to be with? How would you feel at the end of the day?)

I'm in our holiday home with my wife and son. It's a warm summer day. I enjoy a few hours alone with my wife. Later, we take a walk along the beach with our son, and stop off at the neighbourhood restaurant for breakfast. I have a game of golf with my best friend in the morning. On the way to the golf course, I listen to my favourite Optimal Thinking cassette tape. I also listen to my favourite music. I pop into the office — near our holiday house — for a few hours and finalise the biggest transaction ever. It is easy and enjoyable. I am in complete control. I then spend an hour with my present team, supervising the production of the highest budget video we've ever produced, for my favourite clients. I celebrate with my wife and son in the late afternoon. We go shopping together and buy whatever we want. We then go home, and have our favourite people over for dinner. We talk and laugh and watch a Marx Brothers video. My wife and I go for a quiet walk after our guests leave. We go to bed happily and peacefully, knowing tomorrow will be better than today.

14. What is my Optimal environment like?

My Optimal environment is our present holiday home with some modifications. We have an extra hectare of land, beautifully landscaped, with the best lighting arrangements. We have an Olympic size swimming pool. We have a view of the ocean from the living room. I have a workshop downstairs, which converts into a ballroom, so we can have large parties. My study is twice its present size. I have my personal gym downstairs decked out with all the latest workout equipment. My son's room is about twice as large as it is now.

15. Which one purpose would I concentrate on if I knew that there was no chance of failure?

Provide the best of everything for my family.

16. What is my Optimal purpose? What do I most want to accomplish?

(Write a one-to-three sentence statement about the main purpose of your life. You may like to combine several responses into an overall statement.)

To feel happy because my life is worthwhile. To be an example of integrity, love and Optimal Thinking for my family and provide them with the best of everything.

When Jack finally wrote out the statement which defined his main purpose in life he felt like a new man. He was filled with joy. He knew this was exactly what he wanted. It felt completely right to him. There was nothing missing!

How do you feel now that you have identified your Optimal purpose in life?

Now that you are aware of your Optimal purpose, as an Optimal Thinker you can simply choose the most positive actions to stay focused on your purpose and minimise distractions. You can ask:

Is this action in alignment with my purpose?
What's the best action I can take right now to fulfil my purpose?

OPTIMAL AFFIRMATIONS

What I truly want is clear to me now.

▼

I am now taking the best action to fulfil my Optimal purpose.

▼

I am now making the best use of my greatest skills.

▼

I am now optimising my best and most beneficial skills.

▼

I invest my time, talents, abilities and life in those activities which fulfil my Optimal purpose and deserve my best efforts.

▼

I concentrate on what I most want to do and what I do best.

DEVELOPING THE SKILLS NECESSARY TO OPTIMISE PURPOSEFUL ACTIVITY

To fulfil your Optimal purpose in the best possible way, you will need the most appropriate skills. You may already have them. If your Optimal purpose is to provide financially for your family, then you must have the skills necessary to command the income you desire. If you wish to be Optimally productive, you may need to acquire Optimal time management skills. If you wish to relate to others as skilfully as possible, it may be wise to attend an Optimal Communication Skills workshop.

You may be aware of only one or two skills necessary to align yourself with your Optimal purpose. That's fine. As you move towards fulfilling your Optimal purpose, any additional skills required will become apparent.

Are you willing to do whatever is necessary to fulfil your Optimal purpose? Below are some questions Jack answered candidly. Take some time to write down your answers to the same questions and make your Optimal commitment to yourself.

1. How much time am I willing to commit to my Optimal purpose daily?
Every moment

2. Is it worthy of my best efforts?
Yes

3. Why?
Because what I really want out of life is to realise my Optimal purpose. I know I will be happy if I stay on track. It feels 100 per cent right!

How did you answer the above questions? Are you fully committed to developing the best skills and taking the best actions to achieve your Optimal purpose? Are you willing to continually ask yourself 'What's the best action I can take right now to fulfil my Optimal purpose?' or will you allow yourself to be overcome by distractions? Remember, all distractions are equal!

We all experience disappointment and become distracted from time to time. Decide to accept your situation and use the following Optimal statements: 'I can have exactly what I want. I can fulfil my Optimal purpose! What's the best action I can take right now?' *Acceptance* followed by the *best action* provides the Optimal strategy for achieving your Optimal purpose.

At the end of each day, you can also monitor yourself by asking 'To what extent are my actions leading me towards the fulfilment of my purpose?'

The next chapter will help you to set goals and plan your best action steps. Optimal Thinkers know where they want to go and the best way to get there. They have goals which provide the best means to achieve their Optimal purpose.

You can choose your Optimal purpose, fulfil it and enjoy what you truly want. When you make the best use of your skills and apply Optimal Thinking to achieve your Optimal purpose you will become who you really want to be, do what you really want to do and have what you really want to have! And then, how will you feel?

CHAPTER FOUR

OPTIMAL PLANNING

I know the best way to achieve my most important goal.
Optimal Thinker

SETTING SUPREME GOALS

Are you ready to give yourself the best of life? It is your right to choose the people you most want to associate with, the city you wish to live in and the career you are most suited for. It is your right to choose, plan and experience your desired reality!

SUPREME goals provide the concrete checkpoints required for the achievement of your Optimal purpose. Optimal Thinkers set

Specific

Uplifting

Paramount

Reachable

Exciting

Measurable

Enjoyable

goals to be achieved within definite time frames.

SUPREME goals are
Specific
Your goals must be stated specifically so that uncertainty and conjecture are eliminated. Specific goals produce specific outcomes. Vague goals produce vague outcomes or no outcome at all. Goals such as to have a fine income, be a caring partner and have peace of mind are useless. $100 000 gross income per year, make special time three nights a week to be alone with Ron, or play nine holes of golf every Tuesday morning are specific goals.

Uplifting

When your goals are uplifting, the rewards you enjoy by achieving them triumph over any price you have to pay. Achieving these SUPREME goals enables you to experience greatest satisfaction and joy.

Paramount

Paramount goals reflect your Optimal *personal* values, needs and wants and require your best efforts to achieve them. They inspire you to be your best, do your best and experience the best life has to offer. They are not based on competition with others.

Reachable

Your goals must be realistic and attainable. When you believe that you can achieve your goals, you are motivated to accomplish them.

Exciting

There is no excitement in just getting by or in mediocrity. Making the house payments and paying your telephone bills will not make life exciting for you. Big goals are exciting and challenge you to do your best. When your goals are exciting you automatically experience an intense desire to achieve them.

Measurable

Your goals are most effective when you can measure their achievement. When your SUPREME goals are scheduled within definite time frames, you have checkpoints to measure your progress. There is no need for wishful thinking because you have observable evidence that they are attainable.

Enjoyable

Optimal Thinkers bring joy to their goals rather than attempt to extract it from them. Enjoyable goals are the tangible results of the joy you bring to them. Interestingly, what you enjoy doing is generally what you're best at.

Jim wants to enjoy more romance in his marriage. Lately he and his wife have been taking each other for granted. He wrote down three SUPREME goals to achieve his purpose.

1. Every three to five days, send Pam a different card to express my love and appreciation.

2. Present Pam with a dozen red roses next Friday.

3. Schedule a candle-light dinner for two in our favourite restaurant to celebrate the end of every month.

WHY PLAN OPTIMALLY?

Many people complain of lack of time and resources when lack of direction is their real problem. They don't know exactly where they want to go and arrive where they don't want to be.

An elderly doctor was called out one morning to deliver a baby. On his way to the hospital he noticed the grass was very dry, so he detoured towards his house to turn on the sprinklers. As he picked up the paper he noticed an advertisement for a play he wished to attend, so he tore it out and placed it on the dining room table where he would be sure to notice it. On the dining room table he noticed several dirty dishes, so he went to the sink to wash them. There, he noticed another pile of dishes and proceeded to wash them too. And finally, in desperation, his wife went to the hospital and delivered the baby.

SUPREME goals provide the Optimal path to achieving your purpose. You make Optimal use of your greatest assets, resources and time when you take the best actions towards your SUPREME goals.

Do you make any of the following statements?

What am I doing here?

Constant interruptions prevent me from getting things done.

I have numerous responsibilities. It's hard to attend to everything.

I don't know how to get what I want. I feel like I'm going around in circles.

I don't feel motivated.

There's just too much to do.

I can't rely on others. I often end up doing everything myself.

These statements are based on less than Optimal planning of your resources and time!

The objective of Optimal Planning is to enable you to achieve your SUPREME goals and Optimal purpose in the best way. An Optimal plan gives you assurance that your SUPREME goals can be achieved. It provides you with the best possible map or blueprint for your success. When you plan Optimally you make things happen on purpose instead of relying on circumstance or chance.

THE VALUE OF WRITTEN SUPREME GOALS

In 1973, the results of a survey revealed some enlightening information about the value of written goals. In 1953, a group of graduating students at Yale university were asked a series of questions, which included, 'Have you set clear, specific goals for your life? Have you written them down and have you made plans to accomplish them?' Three per cent of those interviewed had written down their goals and formulated specific plans to attain them. Twenty years later the surviving members of that class were again interviewed. The 3 per cent who had written down their goals had achieved greater financial success than the entire other 97 per cent. The students had originally been chosen because of their similar family and socioeconomic backgrounds, intelligence, academic ability and even physical appearance. The only visible difference between the successful 3 per cent and the others was that they had written down their goals and plans.

Do you believe that major corporations such as IBM or Mercedes-Benz would experience the same success if their Directors had the corporate goals in mind rather than written down?

Writing down your SUPREME goals serves to clarify your thinking and gives you clarity of purpose. It also provides an Optimal track for your progress. You know exactly what you must do next to achieve what you want. By frequently referring to your written SUPREME goals you can minimise distractions and interruptions. You generate more time to do what you really want to do. You also gain clear mental pictures of exactly what you want. This stimulates the visualisation process which hastens your progress towards your goals. Conflicts also become apparent and you can focus on resolving them before they become serious problems. Writing down your SUPREME goals can even help you communicate clearly to others what you consider most important.

MODES OF OPTIMAL PLANNING

There are two modes of Optimal planning: forward planning and reverse planning. It is important to balance their use. Remember, only when you implement your Optimal plan will you experience success.

Optimal forward planning

If you knew where you wanted to go and had the best map to show you how to get there, would you arrive at your chosen destination if you didn't know where you were? The answer to this question is an obvious no. When you know where you stand now, you have the basis for determining exactly where you want to go and how to get there.

In the forward planning process you start from where you are. *You move forward as far as you can see, and when you arrive at that point you look further.* You write down your SUPREME goals in order of priority and then move into action. You continually ask yourself 'What is the most important goal I must achieve?' and 'What's the best action I can take towards it right now?'

We all differ when it comes to planning ahead. Some people have no difficulty setting short, medium and long term goals. They plan years ahead. Others plan to achieve SUPREME goals several months ahead. Some can only plan a few days in advance. Some people consider short term to be sixty days, medium term six months and long term two years. Others use completely different time frames. What do you consider to be short, medium and long term? How far ahead do you plan?

Setting and achieving short term SUPREME goals optimises your confidence and builds the habit of taking the best path to achieve your success. Each experience of success forms the foundation for more.

Lisa, a 39-year-old financial planning consultant, works from home. She is very competent and professional in her business dealings. A lot of her energy goes into making her business a success. Lisa's struggle is internal. Lisa has been divorced for seven years and has not had a serious relationship since. She feels sad, disappointed and angry about her barren personal life. Although she has never had a strong, persistent desire to have children, she wonders whether she has missed her chance. Her business is suffering.

When Lisa wrote down her goals she made sure every sentence was Optimally stated. Lisa's list of SUPREME goals for the next two months in order of priority, was as follows:

1. After work this evening write a list of the most important characteristics I would like in my future mate.

6.00 p.m. 10 April

2. Write a list in my diary of my ten best business prospects to contact each day.

5.35 p.m. nightly starting 10 April

3. Schedule three business meetings daily.

10 a.m., 12 noon and 3 p.m. starting 11 April

4. Utilise Optimal Thinking each morning for twenty minutes to prepare me for an Optimal day.

Every day at 7.30 a.m. starting 11 April

5. Write in journal every morning 'I can have exactly what I want', for ten minutes after Optimal Thinking.

Every day at 7.50 a.m. starting 11 April

6. Schedule five hours next week to investigate the best places to meet the most appropriate single men.

13 April, 7-10 p.m. and 15 April, 6-8 p.m.

7. Invest four evenings each week in the most uplifting singles environments or with suitable male prospects.

Tuesdays, Thursdays, Fridays, Saturdays

8. Attend weekend seminar on relationships.

1 and 2 May

9. Attend National Financial Planning conference.

11 May

Which SUPREME goals do you wish to achieve in the near and more distant future? Write them down and take some time NOW to plan ahead. You deserve it!

Optimal reverse planning

In the Optimal reverse planning process, you break down your Optimal dreams and SUPREME goals into realistic action steps. You begin by writing an Optimal dream/goal list. Dreams are those desires which do not have a clear series of steps attached to their fulfilment. Never judge or discount them. Your dreams are real and meaningful to you. They become goals when you clearly define the specific actions necessary to achieve them.

A goal set impulsively and casually entertained is often discarded at the first obstacle. When you reverse plan, you can decide if your goal is worthwhile before involving yourself in the activities necessary for its accomplishment. If you decide that the benefits will bring out the best in you, inspire the fulfilment of your Optimal purpose and triumph over the price you will have to pay, you have reason to proceed. Many times I plan out the fulfilment of a dream and discover that it isn't currently worthy. I simply discard the piece of paper and abandon the project, or file it for later consideration. Reverse planning eliminates the time wastage caused by trial and error.

Below are some Optimal questions to assist you in the process of reverse planning. Take some time to write down your responses.

1. List my Optimal dreams and SUPREME goals. What do I most want to be, do, have and contribute? Which dreams and goals are worthy of my best efforts? Which goals will assist me most to achieve my Optimal purpose?

Here it is important to jot down whatever comes to mind. Let go of any judgements or self-imposed limitations. Put those dreams down on paper. If you could be anyone you wanted, who would you be? A politician? A leading physician? A film director? An athlete? A business magnate? An accomplished artist? A spiritual master? Sit yourself down in a quiet place and let yourself go. Remember the greatest inventions and developments in history came from the minds of dreamers who made their dreams come true. You can do it too.

John Goddard did it. At fifteen years of age John wrote a list of 127 things he wanted to achieve in his life. He wanted to climb Mount Everest, run a five-minute mile, read the Bible, write a book, read the *Encyclopaedia Britannica* from cover to cover and visit every country in the world, amongst other things.

John Goddard, now middle-aged, has already reached 105 of his 127 goals. He is still enthusiastic about visiting the twenty-eight countries he hasn't seen yet, going to the moon, living in the twenty-first century, and realising many more of the exciting goals on his list.

Are you ready to identify the dreams that will bring out the best in you? The question 'Why haven't I achieved my Optimal purpose already?' will assist you to identify the SUPREME goals you must achieve to fulfil your Optimal purpose. What are they?

2. Which one is most important?
Now look at your list. Which one would you dare to accomplish if you knew you couldn't fail? Decide which one is of Optimal importance to you.

PLATINUM RULE: It is unwise to share your goal before you have planned its accomplishment with those who are not supportive. Others can destroy your enthusiasm with comments like: 'It won't work!' 'That's unrealistic' or 'You're crazy!' Share your goal only with those who will assist you to achieve it.

3. List the rewards that will optimise my desire to achieve my SUPREME goal. What are all the benefits to be gained? Why is it of utmost importance that I reach it? How will I feel?

You are probably familiar with the Law of Inertia. It states: 'A body at rest will remain at rest and a body in motion will continue to move in the same direction at the same speed unless acted upon by an external force.' This law can be stated even more simply: 'If you do what you've always done, you'll have what you've always had'. Those who achieve their goals, continue achieving their goals, those who think negatively continue thinking negatively and those who struggle with life continue to struggle. The benefits to be enjoyed by achieving your SUPREME goal provide the force required to change and optimise the speed and direction of your path. These benefits will triumph over your inertia when you give of your best to attain them.

To optimise your motivation, give yourself as many uplifting reasons as possible to proceed. Why do I want it? What's in it for me? What are all the benefits? How will I feel? Keep reminders closeby of all the benefits you will enjoy by achieving your goal.

4. Write down where I am now in relation to my goal.

Martha's SUPREME goal was to weigh fifty-five kilograms (120 pounds) within two months. To define where she was in relation to her goal, her first task was to note her current weight.

Irwin wanted to earn $1000 a week. When he looked at last week's commission cheque, he knew where he stood in relation to his SUPREME goal.

Where do you stand right now in relation to your SUPREME goal?

5. Possible obstacles: if this is what I want most, why don't I have it already?

Mary, a 38-year-old psychologist, wants to teach psychology at university level. She believes she isn't sufficiently qualified. She doesn't have a Ph.D. To gain a Ph.D at least two years of additional study are necessary, and several thousand dollars which she doesn't have.

Jim, forty-one, wants his own radio talk show. The only credit he can put on his resumé is a ten-minute interview he conducted recently with a reasonably well-known friend. He feels he lacks presentation skills, experience and the right connections.

Catherine, forty-two, wants to open a day care centre for children, but she doesn't have enough money.

Qualifications, attitude, experience and *money* are the most common obstacles which frustrate our success. But with determination, initiative and Optimal Thinking, you can overcome them.

In 1933 after Fred Astaire's first screen test the following memo was written by an MGM director.

'Can't act! Slightly bald! Can dance a little.'

After several years as head of the secondary science department, a young teacher was ready to take on a new challenge. She had noticed an advertisement in the daily newspaper for language consultants. International travel was mentioned. She enjoyed languages, communicating with others and travel.

She had four major obstacles to overcome. Firstly, she did not have any significant educational qualifications in languages. Her prospective employer assured her that this was not necessary. Consultants were trained extensively by the company on the 'how to's' of learning languages. Secondly, she had a negative attitude about sales. She did not like the idea of being a sales person. As she considered herself an educator, she resolved to continue viewing herself as such. Her complete dedication to the educational value of the programs could only be to the advantage of all concerned. Thirdly, she had no sales experience. She was told that the corporate training empowered consultants to discuss the programs with people at all levels. No experience was required. Finally, this was a commission only job and offered no financial security. She had always received a salary and was uncomfortable starting out in a new venture without any financial backing. She asked her prospective employer to provide her with a salary for three months. He agreed to match her previous salary for three months and they decided to give it a go.

There were fifty consultants in the company. She asked about the best consultant. What was his background? What kind of results was he achieving? Why was he successful? She discovered that the top consultant was a charming man in his late fifties, who suffered various physical ailments. This man had been successful in real estate prior to becoming a language consultant. He was exceptional. She was not expected to achieve his level of success. She thought: 'I am young, healthy, energetic, and have a sound educational foundation. If he can do it, I can!'

Numerous obstacles crossed her path during her first month. She persisted and gave the tasks at hand everything she had. By the end of that month, she had reached her personal goals, doubled her previous income and was the company's top language consultant. That young girl was me!

> **Obstacles are the things we see when we take our eyes off our goal.**
>
> **Obstacles are the things we hear when we take our ears off our goal.**
>
> **Obstacles are the things we think when we take our mind off our goal.**
>
> **Obstacles are what we feel when we take our heart off our goal.**

If there were no obstacles in your path, you would have already achieved your goal. Why don't you have your SUPREME goal right now? What's in the way? Take some time now to write down your obstacles.

6. Optimal solutions: what's the best action I can take to overcome these obstacles?

When you fight shadows or move in the dark it's hard to forge ahead. It is best to throw light on your obstacles. Accept them, take the best actions you can to overcome them and persist toward your SUPREME goal. *Acceptance followed by the best possible action will work every time.*

Esther, a sales person, knew that recognition of her best efforts was of utmost importance to her. She was ambitious and wanted to become a manager. She was the top producer for the company in her first year, but her employer chose not to mention her achievements at the national awards meeting. He even promoted someone else above her. She felt hurt and disillusioned. Her productivity drastically declined.

To overcome this obstacle Esther acknowledged that this employer did not value her best efforts. She decided that her best course of action was to seek another job where her work would be appreciated. She found a similar position and quickly rose to the top. In her new position she was respected by all those who knew her. At the end of her first year she accepted

OPTIMAL AFFIRMATIONS

I am now taking the best actions to accomplish my most important goal.

▼

I am making the best use of my time right now.

▼

I am making the most profitable use of my time right now.

▼

The fastest route to my SUPREME goal is my Optimal plan.

▼

I give all that I have to attain my most important goals.

▼

I am making the most of every moment.

an offer from her new employer to head a new division as sales manager.

Negative thinking, procrastination and feelings such as fear, worry, doubt, guilt, hurt and anger can cripple your progress. Optimal Thinkers are as human as everyone else. They experience negative thoughts and feelings but overcome them with minimum time loss using Optimal Thinking. When less than Optimal thinkers experience the same negative thoughts and feelings, they stay off track for longer periods and don't bounce back to their Optimal level.

When you become conscious of negative thoughts or feelings, simply accept them and then choose to think Optimally. Ask yourself the best questions, listen to your inner voice for the best answers and then incorporate your solutions into your Optimal plan. Ask 'What's the best use of my time right now?' 'What's the best action I can take now?' or 'Which SUPREME goal must I focus on right now?'

7. Optimal resources: what are my greatest strengths?
Which organisations and people, and what information, can most assist me to achieve my SUPREME goal?

Optimal Thinkers build their greatest strengths into their Optimal plan to achieve their purpose. Optimal leaders discover and acknowledge the strengths of their people and encourage their full expression. Take some time now to itemise the best resources available to achieve your SUPREME goal. Make sure you list them in order of their importance to you.

8. Optimal action steps: in priority with target times

Optimal action steps, such as asking the best person in your field for advice or reading the most enlightening literature about an item you wish to purchase, provide the Optimal path to your SUPREME goals. These are the best steps you can take to maximise your momentum. You might like to think about each action step and ask 'What will make this most pleasurable/profitable/time efficient?' Transfer your list of Optimal action steps into your daily calendar to remind you when to take action. As you work on your Optimal plan, the best of life will unfold.

9. What is the Optimal time frame for the completion of my SUPREME goal?

It is now realistic to set an Optimal time frame for the completion of your SUPREME goal. Optimal time frames motivate you to employ your best efforts to do what's necessary to get the job done. Time frames change the operational value of your plan from 'it can be accomplished one of these days' to 'it will be accomplished by the best date'. Be flexible. If you do not achieve your goal within the stated time, simply extend the target date. Make sure you are the master of time and time is not the master of you!

10. Are all the benefits to be gained worth the price I'll have to pay? Is this SUPREME goal worthy of my complete commitment (emotionally, financially, energetically and otherwise)?

Be entirely honest with yourself now. The answer to this question will determine your commitment to implement your Optimal plan. The strength of your desire and commitment to your goal is paramount.

11. What's the first step I must take to activate this plan?

Identify the first Optimal action step you will take to achieve your goal and *DO IT NOW!*

12. Which Optimal affirmations will optimise the accomplishment of my goal?

The use of Optimal self-talk is an Optimal verbal application of 'act as if'. Many Optimal Thinkers use the following statement: 'I am now taking the best action to accomplish my most important goal'.

Some prefer to mention the benefits of achieving their goal in their Optimal affirmations. Which Optimal affirmations are most appropriate for you? Take some time to write them down now.

13. Which Optimal visualisations will optimise the accomplishment of my SUPREME goal?

Colonel Johnson was an enthusiastic golfer whose score was consistently around ninety. He stopped playing golf for eight years. The next time he played eighteen holes of golf, he shot a seventy-five.

For those eight years Colonel Johnson had been a prisoner of war in Vietnam. He had been isolated from others that whole time. Initially he feared for his sanity but after a few months he decided to take total control of his mind. He set a SUPREME goal to achieve a score of seventy-five when he next played eighteen holes of golf at his favourite course. Each day he mentally played his best game of golf for four hours. Through visualisation he chose his favourite golf course, dressed himself in his best golfing clothes and approached the tee every morning. He paced himself as though he were physically present on the golf course. He noted the weather as he put the ball down. He viewed in complete detail, the green grass, the slopes, the trees and everything else which would affect his game. He made sure that he held his club correctly and visualised himself swing and follow through on each shot. He watched the ball fly down the fairway, hit the ground and roll to the exact spots he aimed for. Colonel Johnson played eighteen holes of his best golf every day for eight years. He saw himself score seventy-five every time. It is no wonder that when he did finally reach his favourite golf course eight years later, his score was seventy-five.

Optimal visualisation is an Optimal mental application of 'act as if'. Are you ready to create a vivid mental picture of exactly what you want? Make the best use of drawings, photos, pictures and other visual aids to assist you in visualising your SUPREME goals.

14. How do I know I'm on track? How can I most effectively monitor my progress?

When you monitor your progress, your confidence and desire to accomplish your SUPREME goal is optimised. Keeping records will assist you to gain an accurate picture of how far you've come, your best results, strengths, weaknesses and more. You can use your daily calendar, diagrams, graphs, ledgers, flow charts and other Optimal tracking devices. You may choose to monitor the achievement of your goals by using lists. What is the best action you can take to monitor your progress right now?

HOW TO MAKE THE BEST USE OF A DAILY CALENDAR

A daily calendar or planner will help you achieve your SUPREME goals. At the beginning of each year, quarter, month, week and day, make sure your SUPREME goals are written down. Break your long term goals and projects down into monthly, weekly and daily goals. Break these goals down into manageable Optimal action steps and place all the steps into your daily calendar.

Every evening, consider your most important activities for the following day. Ask yourself: 'What's the best way to optimise my day? What must I do to make the most of it? What are the most important goals I must achieve?' Write down your activities for the following day. Prioritise the imperative tasks with an 'A', then the important tasks with a 'B'. Activities which are not important but could be useful are best noted with a 'C'. You may rate a task as a B and discover it's really a less important C. This will become apparent in time. If you have many As, Bs and Cs, write 'A1', 'A2', 'A3', 'A4', 'B1', 'B2' etc. alongside your planned activities. Make sure you consider how long each task will take so that you can enjoy an achievable schedule.

Many people fail to keep to their schedules or implement their plans because they underestimate the amount of time they invest reacting to unexpected and urgent issues. Bear in mind how much reactive time is usual in your situation. Look at your last week or a realistic time frame, to discover the ratio of your 'proactive' or planned time to reactive time. Keep this in mind when organising your daily schedule. Set yourself up for Optimal productivity each and every day.

Jane, a freelance writer, writes best in the mornings. In the afternoons, she finds it difficult to come up with new ideas. Do you find you are more productive at certain times of the day than others? If so, simply schedule the activities which require your greatest productivity for those times. Save the other tasks for times when you are less productive.

Remember, you can't do thirty-five hours worth of tasks in fourteen hours. Be realistic. Jack was in the habit of writing thirty to forty tasks on his 'do' list each day. He usually completed about ten of them. He was overwhelmed by all the work which needed to be done. He felt like a failure every day. It was all too much. He desperately needed an experience of success. Jack eventually decided to take charge of his time and life. He began by setting an achievable number of tasks every day, and at the end of each day, he proudly checked off the tasks he had set for himself. Once he was able to feel like a winner on a daily basis, he began to appreciate and enjoy his life.

A journey of a thousand miles does start with a single step. An Optimal daily do list will inspire you to put your best foot forward and challenge you to do your best. At the end of each day you can answer the question: 'How much of my activity contributed to my Optimal purpose today?' You can check off what you've done, or if you don't complete a task on a specific day, simply reschedule and reprioritise it for the next day. You may wish to circle it or place a 'T' next to it (to indicate its transference from day to day) until you complete it. Your calendar provides a checklist of exactly when your goals were set and completed. When you are feeling unproductive a list of completed goals can be your best source of inspiration.

When you go shopping you probably use a list to remind yourself of what you want. While you are walking around do you consider the purchase of other items that appeal to you? You can choose to live your life in this manner. Give yourself some unplanned time every day to enjoy and make the most of any unexpected opportunities. While you're completing the actions on your do list, accept all the opportunities that promote the fulfilment of your Optimal purpose.

It is best to schedule some time every day to do whatever you feel like doing. You can use this time to enjoy your intuition and creativity. Balance planning with spontaneous time.

You can also use your calendar to help you with Optimal affirmations. When you want to integrate an affirmation, for example, 'I am making the most productive use of my time right now' or 'I am doing the most important task right now', jot it down on a transferable sticker, place it on your calendar and move it forward every day. The Post-it™ papers are ideal.

I note my Optimal affirmations on these stickers and am compelled to confront them several times a day. You may wish to use the following affirmations to help you make the best use of your time:

I am making Optimal use of my time right now.

I am making the wisest use of my time right now.

I am making the most productive use of my time right now.

I am making the most profitable use of my time right now.

I am making the most pleasurable use of my time right now.

I am enjoying the most pleasurable path to my goal right now.

I am taking the best action toward my most important goal right now.

I am doing the most important task right now.

I am now fully appreciative of all the value in my life.

I am always punctual.

I obtain the best results within the least amount of time.

Would you like to introduce a new habit into your life? Your calendar can make it easy. Start by reminding yourself of the new desired behaviour every day by placing a transferable sticker on your calendar and move it forward each day.

Not too long ago Debbie decided to resume her program of regular exercise. She had become bored with her previous aerobics program, but hadn't found an adequate, enjoyable substitute. Debbie wrote 'half-hour daily enjoyable aerobic exercise' on a bright sticker on her calendar and moved it along every day. On the first day she ignored it. On the second day she felt guilty. On the third day she felt very guilty. On the fourth day she managed two minutes of a new aerobics program. Soon, Debbie was enjoying thirty minutes of aerobic exercise every day.

Make sure you remind yourself of your plans every day. Place your planner in a position where you can't avoid it. Rodney used his planner erratically at first. He then discovered it was best to complete and double check his lists at night so that his subconscious could prepare him further during sleep. During the day, Rodney writes down the various activities for the following days as they come to his attention. How can you optimise the use of your daily calendar right now?

THE WORST EVENT SCENARIO: RISK TAKING AND PLANNING

Most people fear being homeless, poverty stricken, old, sick and alone. These fears are often irrational. You can minimise them by realising they are based on unreasonable negative thoughts and expectations. When contemplating the worst thing that could happen to you, you face your worst fears. Optimal Thinkers feel their fears and forge ahead regardless, taking the best possible actions.

The worst event scenario is best used when evaluating risks. You look at the worst that could happen should you take the risk. You then formulate an Optimal contingency plan which shows you how to make the best of the worst possible outcome. Once you know how you can handle the worst, you are free to direct all your efforts towards achieving the best outcome.

John was planning a new business. He believed the worst that could happen was that it would fail and he would lose all his money. If this occurred, he resolved to drive a taxi to recoup his financial losses.

When evaluating risks, do you face the worst possible scenario and compile an Optimal contingency plan?

ALTERNATIVE PLANS OF ACTION. WHEN ARE THEY NECESSARY?

It isn't always possible to see clearly into the future. Any Optimal plan you develop is the best you can do at the time. As new circumstances arise and changes occur, updating will be necessary. When you are confronted with unexpected obstacles, alternative plans are essential. We learned how to walk, talk, drive a car, read, write and cook by the principle of *attempt, fail, adjust, attempt again.*

If you are confronted with an unexpected obstacle or change of circumstance, re-evaluate the best outcome. Monitor, update and optimise your plans to take account of the new circumstances. Take the best action to achieve your Optimal end result at every given moment. Where there's a will, there's an Optimal way!

Paul had planned a weekend fishing trip with his son Andrew. On Friday, Andrew broke his arm during a football match. Paul, an Optimal Thinker, asked himself how he could make the most of the weekend. He found himself looking at his list of SUPREME goals. His number one priority was to organise a party for his wife's birthday. He immediately started visualising the Optimal party, and wrote out the guest list. He wrote down an Optimal plan to accomplish his SUPREME goal and moved into action, starting with the highest priority on his list. He knew this weekend would still be an Optimal one!

CHAPTER FIVE

OPTIMISING YOUR FEELINGS

**That action is best which procures the greatest happiness
of the greatest number.**
Francis Hutcheson

THE VALUE OF EMOTIONS

Howard's girlfriend was confused and unhappy. Even though
she explained that her emotional turmoil was not because of
him, Howard felt rejected. When she decided to spend a week
alone to sort out her feelings, he wrote her an abusive letter. She
was hurt and ended the relationship.

Are you ever too angry to be reasonable, too excited to be
logical, or too depressed to think in your best interests? Can you
stay logical and reasonable when your feelings are involved? Do
you view feelings and thoughts as separate and incongruent
parts of yourself?

Your emotional life is a natural part of you. Your feelings are
direct responses to your perception. They signal whether your
experiences are pleasurable or painful. When you experience
your feelings you are in touch with your humanness. When you
honour your feelings you show respect for yourself. Accepting
your vulnerability enables you to confront your weaknesses and
make the most of them.

Cheryl, a warm, articulate woman, had worked in the film
industry for nearly twenty years. Her resumé showed a variety
of positions, yet her status and salary remained mediocre.
Cheryl felt badly that she had not progressed in her career.
Many of her younger colleagues already held top positions and
were taking home gigantic salaries. She had lost her job some
four months ago and was receiving unemployment benefits.

Cheryl was dating a wealthy man who had promised her the
world. Friends often called to invite her for lunch and she

eagerly participated in many varied activities. She did not read the film trade magazines, nor did she go to the movies very often. For several months she made no attempt to find a job. Cheryl's passion for her work was gone. When the relationship with her boyfriend ended, she began to complain of migraine headaches.

One day Jim, an Optimal Thinker and old friend, asked her to read a film script he had just completed. Cheryl couldn't remember being so inspired by a script. Suddenly a light went on inside her. 'This is my opportunity to make a contribution to the world. This script is the basis of an Optimal feature film. I am going to produce it!' She was on top of the world. This was a chance to give her best efforts to a project she really believed in. The next day she called Jim. She was ready to start work.

Our feelings give us direction. Our passion indicates what has meaning or importance for us. Feelings provide the motivation that propels our mind to accomplish its goals. The expertise of a top executive, athlete or entertainer is gained through an intense desire for mastery. We experience our most positive feelings when our most important needs are met.

Optimal Thinking is the vehicle which enables us to take the best route to meet our needs and achieve what is most important to us. It helps us to understand and make the most of our feelings. With Optimal Thinking we can interpret, rationalise, and arrange our feelings into the best perspective.

According to Howard Asher, a psychotherapist,

> We not only have to do what we have to do in life, but we have to feel that what we're doing is in our best interests, in order to feel good about it.

Employing exclusively thinking-based action, or exclusively feelings-based action will not produce the best outcome. We produce the best results when we feel, think and give of our best!

OVERPOWERING EMOTIONS

Have you ever had feelings that were threatening to your sense of security? Anita and Lionel were intensely attracted to each other ten years ago. Anita had suffered tremendous hurt when

Lionel rejected her. All of a sudden he was in her life again. When she heard his voice again for the first time, her heart pounded violently and she struggled to speak articulately.

It's not the presence of emotions that can be detrimental but the inability to incorporate them productively into everyday behaviour. Have you ever asked someone why they are angry only to hear them scream, 'I'm not angry!'? Denying feelings like anger and resentment doesn't allow you to deal with them and can cause them to build up into rage.

Sometimes denial of your feelings protects you in the short term but is counterproductive in the long term.

Peter and Olivia spent a lot of time together but communication was superficial. They both appeared cool and confident. He did not acknowledge his intense feelings for her and she was afraid to express her feelings for him. There was an emotional distance between them because they denied their feelings and didn't deal with them. Do you ever deny what you feel, misrepresent what you see, rationalise, misinterpret, or use pretence to defend yourself?

When there is a strong background emotion such as rage, jealousy or love, your perception and thinking can be distorted. If a mother is seething with anger about her daughter lying to her, she is probably not in the best frame of mind to work out the Optimal plan for future communications. The stronger her emotions, the more likely they are to overpower her reason.

Many people fear the loss of control accompanied by expressing their feelings. All painful feelings, including jealousy, hatred, disappointment, sadness, frustration, worry, embarrassment, discouragement, insecurity and hopelessness, stem from a loss or injury. Are you willing to deal most effectively with the emotions which disturb you?

The disturbing emotions
Hurt

We all feel hurt from time to time. These painful feelings arise when we lose something. The greater the loss, the more profoundly we hurt. You are likely to feel hurt when someone you care about ignores you or is insensitive to your needs. Hurt tells you what is important to you.

Anxiety

Anxiety is fear of future, or the remembrance of past hurt, danger or loss. It can vary in form and intensity and can be real or imagined. You can feel uncertain, edgy, worried, insecure, nervous or even terrified. You sense that something bad is about to happen.

Anger

Anger is a response to suffering hurt or feeling loss. Angry feelings arise when we feel threatened, deprived or unfairly treated. You may experience frustration, irritability, annoyance, resentment or even rage. Sometimes other disturbing emotions accompany anger. When others mistreat you, latent feelings of unworthiness and fear can also be stirred.

Guilt

Healthy guilt occurs when you have hurt or wronged another person or yourself. It occurs when anger is turned inward. You feel undeserving, wrong, stupid, sorry or disappointed in yourself. When you lie to those who trust you, cheat on your partner or blame someone else for something that's your fault, you are liable to feel guilty. This guides you to act in a manner that is in greater alignment with the best person you can be.

When you feel disappointed because you haven't lived up to your own or other's unrealistic expectations, you experience unhealthy guilt which can lead to low self-esteem.

Depression

Depression occurs when hurt and anger are turned inward. When you experience loss, and do not express your feelings about the anger and grief, you will eventually experience depression. Depressed people focus on losses, inner emptiness, unfulfilled dreams, problems and their own worthlessness.

Grief

Grief occurs when we experience a major loss. Feelings such as anger, hurt, dismay, emptiness, sadness and helplessness are evoked.

Elisabeth Kübler-Ross in her research on death and dying identified the following natural stages of the grief process:

1. Denial (This can't be true.)
2. Anger (It's unfair. Why me, why now?)
3. Remorse (If I had not done this, maybe things would be different.)
4. Depression (Helplessness and surrender.)
5. Acceptance (This is the way it is. I will accept and make the most of it.)

Envy

Envy results from feeling deprived, not necessarily because you don't have enough, but because someone else has more. The basis of envy is a feeling of irrational deprivation that signifies dissatisfaction with yourself. Feeling resentful that you don't have what someone else has, distracts you from concentrating on attaining what you want. Your resources are depleted by your resentment.

The best ways to manage feelings

1. Accept your feelings

Are you willing to take five minutes now to experience your internal world? You will need to sit in a comfortable position, close your eyes and notice what happens. Is your inner world dominated by feelings or thoughts? Is there a balance of both? How do you feel right now? What's going on inside you? What emotions are you feeling most strongly?

The more honest you are about your feelings, the more energy you will have to deal with your life. This is the basis of creating happiness in your life. Simply ask yourself: 'What emotions are involved here? What do I feel?'

2. Understand your feelings

Are you ready to minimise the influence of disturbing emotions on your thinking? Like any other threat to your safety, disturbing emotions are handled best when you are clear about what you are confronting.

When you understand your emotions you can better understand the world around you. Your feelings provide you with knowledge and understanding about yourself and others. Many people accept their feelings only after they understand them. For example, when you can identify the various feelings fuelling your anger, you can respond most intelligently. You should first allow yourself to feel the anger then you can validate and appreciate yourself for your willingness to accept and resolve your feelings.

You can optimise your understanding of your feelings by asking yourself the following questions: 'Why do I feel this way? What am I afraid of? Have I felt like this before? What situation, event or person is linked to this feeling? How do I behave when I feel angry/depressed/hurt, etc?'

3. Determine the best way to resolve them

It is important to decide whether to express feelings immediately or contain them until you understand them and work out the best way to resolve them. There are many ways to resolve feelings. You can talk directly to the person involved, write a letter or meditate. You can ask yourself: 'What's the best way to deal with this feeling now? What's the best way to resolve this? What's the best action I can take to achieve what I want?'

For example, to overcome depression, begin by directing energy outward. A schedule of daily activities when acted upon will produce Optimal experiences and feelings as goals are achieved. Expressing your anger will also help.

You can carry a memo book with you and record your negative thoughts. When you feel depressed, combat your negative thinking with Optimal Thinking. Let Optimax give your negative voice a pep talk. Act upon your Optimal thoughts and you will feel renewed and at your best.

Feelings of anxiety are best eliminated by removing the threat that's causing them, not by defensively denying or ignoring it.

Many people threaten themselves by habitually focusing on negative possibilities. You can minimise your anxiety by thinking Optimally. Focus on the best ways to achieve what you want. Ask: 'What am I afraid of losing? What's the best action I can take to prevent the loss and minimise the pain? What's the best action I can take to get what I want?'

It is usually best to express the hurt underlying your anger directly to the person involved. Tell them why you feel angry. Point out how their behaviour is causing you problems and express commitment to finding the best solution for all concerned. Say: 'When you do this, I feel angry/hurt because ... What's the best way we can resolve this?' When you feel guilty, ask yourself: 'What expectations have I disappointed myself with by not living up to them? What's the best way to resolve this?'

Greg, a journalist, felt very annoyed when his boss complained about his latest story. Greg took out a pen and paper and analysed his anger in the following way.

Situation: Boss complained my work was inadequate.

Emotion involved: Anger.

What caused the disturbing emotion? Describe loss, threat or injury: I am afraid my job is at risk because my work is not good enough. I feel my boss shows no respect for my professional abilities when he complains about my work.

Optimal response, best strategy/action to be taken: Take time to understand how the fear originated, and realise that I'm not in the past now.

Acknowledge and remind myself of all my accomplishments. Assess what is in everyone's best interests before writing each new story. Talk to boss. Tell him I will produce the best stories if he points out the flaws *and* the value in my work. I will then be receptive to accepting the flaws and finding the best solutions to overcome them.

Take some time now to think back to your last emotionally disturbing experience. Now with pencil and paper, start examining it, using the format above. Make a few extra charts for yourself and keep them handy. The next time you face an emotionally disturbing situation, take out a chart and use it to examine the situation. Eventually you will form the habit of automatically reviewing each emotionally upsetting situation, analysing and accepting the causes, and responding most intelligently.

WHEN FEELINGS ARE UNMANAGEABLE

If you entered a closed room which was full of gas, it would be best to take the following actions in order of priority:

1. Open the doors and windows to let the gas out.
2. Look for the source of the gas leakage, so you could eliminate it.
3. Decide on the best place to be while the gas is being dispersed.

Similarly, when you are overloaded with disturbing feelings, feeling devastated and out of control, you should:

1. Reduce their influence by giving yourself a cooling off period.
2. Ascertain exactly what is provoking your feelings.
3. Determine the best way to handle them.

To re-establish control of your feelings, involve yourself with manageable activity. You can inhale deeply counting from one to four, then exhale, counting again from one to four. Continue this process until you regain your sense of bodily awareness and a feeling of equanimity. When overwhelmed by your feelings, you can also choose to count to 100, take a walk, go for a run, play the piano or listen to your favourite music. Sometimes I visualise my angry feelings as a pot of boiling water which I take off the burner to cool down. Involve yourself with something you can do by yourself and for yourself so that you are in control. When you have regained your composure, you can then look at what the disturbed feelings were all about. Where did they come from? What provoked them? What's the best way to deal with them?

WHEN FEELINGS ARE MANAGEABLE

If you entered a closed room which was slightly filled with gas, it would be best to take the following actions in order of priority:

1. Look for the source of the gas leakage, so you can eliminate it.

2. Open the doors and windows to let the gas out.

3. Decide on the best place to be while the gas is being dispersed.

Similarly, if you are feeling slightly agitated about something you can:

1. Ascertain exactly what is provoking your feelings.

2. Reduce their influence by giving yourself the opportunity to calm down.

3. Determine the best way to handle them.

Ask: 'Why am I feeling so bad? What precipitated this feeling? What's the best way to deal with it? What's the best action I can take to achieve what I want right now?'

Mary, an experienced and highly respected professional, was conducting a seminar series and achieving top results. Paul, an unknown seminar leader, who considered himself a champion in the same field, was attending her seminars. He appeared to be happy with the seminars, and shared with the other participants numerous stories of the benefits he had gained. He even called Mary's office and asked to be included on her staff. Mary explained gently that there were no positions currently available and advised him to send his resumé to her for future consideration.

During the coffee break at the next seminar, Paul confronted Mary and told her that her seminars were the worst he had ever attended. He pointed out all the flaws in her presentation and accused her of lack of professionalism. He concluded the confrontation by informing her that he was the best in this field.

Mary was disturbed by Paul's attack. She asked herself: 'Why am I upset? What's the best action I can take to resolve my feelings about this?' She realised that although she felt hurt that Paul did not appreciate her best efforts, this confrontation was unimportant in terms of what she had set out to accomplish. The nasty words of a jealous competitor simply weren't worth wasting time over. She resolved to get on with the seminar and do the best she knew how.

HOW DO YOU RELATE TO YOUR FEELINGS?

Below are several statements to help you gain insight into how you relate to your feelings. In each sentence there is space allotted for you to add one of the following words: always, often, usually, sometimes, rarely, never.

After each statement write the best action you can take to improve yourself.

1. I .... accept my feelings.

2. I .... respect the feelings of others.

3. I .... listen to both my mind and my heart.

4. I .... resolve my feelings of hurt in the best possible way.

5. I .... resolve my feelings of anxiety in the best possible way.

6. I .... resolve my feelings of anger in the best possible way.

7. I .... resolve my feelings of guilt in the best possible way.

8. I .... resolve my feelings of depression in the best possible way.

9. I .... feel confident.

10. I .... trust myself.

11. I .... feel joyful.

12. I .... feel loving.

13. I .... understand my feelings.

14. I am .... confident that I deal with my feelings in the best possible ways.

15. When I lose control of my feelings I .... take some time to cool down and regain my composure.

16. I .... forgive myself and others easily.

17. I .... count my blessings.

18. I .... use Optimal Thinking.

19. I .... visualise myself at my best enjoying exactly what I want.

20. I .... relax and meditate on Optimal experiences and feelings.

21. I .... laugh.

22. I .... verbalise my emotions with other Optimal Thinkers.

23. I .... do my best.

If your response to any statement was:

Always, your attitude and skills in that area are Optimal — congratulations!

Often or *usually*, your attitude and skills are extraordinary, close to Optimal. It will be easy for you to bridge the gap.

Sometimes, your attitude and skills are mediocre. Are you ready to take Optimal actions to rectify this?

Rarely or *never*, this is a negative area for you. Are you willing and ready to take Optimal steps to rectify this right now? You do deserve to have exactly what you want!

HOW TO OPTIMISE YOUR FEELINGS

To optimise your most positive feelings, discover which needs are being met when you experience them. How are they met? What are your most important needs and what's the best way you can satisfy them? Optimal Thinking is a tool which can be used to create those situations, circumstances and events where your most beneficial emotions can be felt.

1. Forgiveness

Forgiveness acknowledges the choice against being the judge and jury over yourself and those who have hurt you. When you forgive, you relieve yourself of the burden of carrying around hurt, anger, pain and loneliness. Healing occurs. When you demonstrate forgiveness, you recall only the positive elements of the situation. When you make compassion a higher priority than judgement it becomes easy to forgive!

2. Gratitude

The more you appreciate what you have, the more you will have to appreciate. When you take the time to count your blessings, you accrue Optimal feelings. Invest a few minutes every morning in gratitude, and at night, acknowledge what you received that day. Start with what you appreciate most about your life. Recognise and appreciate the best in yourself, others and the world. Learn to appreciate and celebrate it all!

3. Self-confidence

Do you feel confident in your day to day life? Do you feel that you have what it takes to achieve what you want? You can optimise your self-confidence by making a list of all the things you do best. Determine how you can make the most of your greatest talents, abilities and accomplishments. When you give yourself credit for what you do best and expect the best of yourself, you will create an environment for optimising your feelings. Remember to always reinforce your accomplishments and triumphs by celebrating them.

Goethe, philosopher and poet, wrote, 'As soon as you trust yourself, you know how to live.' Trust stems from confidence in your ability to deal with the circumstances you encounter. When you are able to trust, you can allow yourself to explore new viewpoints. Trust encourages you to be open to new experiences and all feelings.

4. Joy and love

When you give love without calculation or expectation of anything in return, you will optimise the feelings of joy, love, confidence and trust in your life. You can then guide yourself into experiences that encourage your most beneficial emotions to thrive. Your greatest bursts of creativity, for example, will most likely occur during joyful moments when you are most willing to experiment and spread your wings. Leo Tolstoy wrote, 'Art is a human activity having for its purpose the transmission to others of the highest and best feelings to which men have risen.' Joy is a signal of Optimal functioning.

5. Optimal affirmations

Make it your business to talk Optimally to yourself at every given moment. Give Optimax complete freedom to triumph over all your Other Voices. By using Optimal affirmations you can create an emotional climate of self-confidence, where your most positive feelings can flourish. Abraham Lincoln said,

'Most people are about as happy as they make up their minds to be.' You can make up your mind to be happy regardless of your circumstances right now.

6. Optimal visualisation

Optimal visualisation enables you to obtain a clear picture of your most important goals and the feelings associated with their accomplishment. You can choose to view, and feel, what it's like to be your best. You can create Optimal feelings by employing words with Optimal emotional content.

Danielle was ready to invest in her dream home. She experienced Optimal feelings every day by imagining herself living happily in her favourite home on the beach. Daily she visualised herself happily strolling along the shore, feeling the warm sand under her feet. She saw her home in detail. She visualised herself confidently furnishing each room. She imagined herself enjoying quiet nights there, and joyfully entertaining her favourite people. She saw herself engaged in activities where she gave of her best. She listened to the waves pounding against the shore, watched the seagulls and felt the serenity and joy of having done all that was necessary to attain her heart's greatest desire. Four months later, Danielle found and bought her dream home.

7. Alpha (self-hypnosis)

When you slow down your brainwave activity to eight to thirteen cycles per second, you enter a hypnotic state of relaxed receptivity called Alpha. Once you are in the Alpha state, you can access your subconscious mind to empower your Optimal self.

You can reach Alpha by imagining your mind completely calm, relaxed and peaceful, as you visualise the colours red, then purple and, finally, blue. Next, slowly count down from twenty-one to zero, feeling the relaxation spread throughout your entire body. Then place yourself in your favourite passive scene of nature. You may choose the seaside, a mountain retreat or a beautiful garden. You can then program your subconscious mind by combining creative visualisation and Optimal affirmations. Imagine the feelings associated with being and doing your best!

OPTIMAL AFFIRMATIONS

I am willing to accept all my feelings.

▼

I am willing to understand all my feelings.

▼

I am always confident that I deal with my feelings in the best possible way.

▼

I always resolve disturbing feelings in the best way.

▼

I take the best actions to resolve my feelings of hurt, anger, guilt, anxiety and depression.

I am willing to be happy.

▼

My life is now filled with pleasure.

▼

I am now in my Optimal state.

▼

I trust myself completely.

▼

I love myself unconditionally.

▼

This is the best day of my life.

▼

I feel my best when I do my best.

When you are in the Optimal Alpha state, form a circle with your right thumb and the first two fingers of your right hand. Once you have made this conscious-unconscious connection, you can utilise this three-finger connection to achieve instant relaxation and connection with your Optimal self. Whenever you use the three-finger connection, you will enter the Alpha state, feeling completely calm, relaxed and in your Optimal state.

You were given a post-hypnotic suggestion while you were in the Alpha state. Frederick Michaels, a hypnotherapist, uses other post-hypnotic suggestions. When his clients are in the hypnotic state, he suggests words like 'white dove' which they can then repeat whenever they wish to re-enter the peaceful hypnotic state.

8. Relaxation and meditation

If you are highly anxious, you need to learn to relax. To relax completely, make sure you are entirely comfortable, regulate your breathing and do visualisation exercises to eliminate muscle tension.

Marilyn Winfield, creative visualisation specialist, suggests the following exercise.

Take three deep breaths, holding on the inhale. Now visualise a silky smooth liquid of relaxation and sense it entering your toes. As it does, feel the toes relaxing. Sense each muscle, each fibre, and each and every cell relaxing. Allow this soothing, healing relaxation to flow up into the pelvic area, the abdomen, the solar plexus and into the torso. As the feeling of relaxation reaches the torso, sense it splashing down the arms, filling up the palms of the hands, the wrists and the fingers into the fingertips. The relaxation permeates your shoulders and neck and fills your head and face. Every muscle in your body is now bathing in silky smooth, soothing relaxation.

Meditation is an Optimal form of relaxation. You may like to sit comfortably, close your eyes and meditate on an Optimal feeling, such as joy, peace, serenity, fun, Optimal self-esteem, compassion, love, strength or laughter. Choose the feeling you most wish to embody, and repeat the word continually to yourself. You can meditate on the meaning it holds for you, and how to make the best use of it in your life.

When other thoughts cross your mind accept them, and as soon as possible, return to embracing your Optimal word. When you experience any other feelings or bodily sensations, simply accept them, and refocus your attention on your Optimal word. The more you meditate on the feeling you wish to embrace, the more you will embrace it. It is best to schedule twenty minutes a day, before meals, to enjoy this relaxing and fulfilling process.

9. Recall Optimal emotional experiences

Can you recall in detail a place, time or circumstance where you felt your very best? When you frequently recall your most pleasurable experiences, you reinforce your Optimal emotional state. Be sure to turn up the light, colour, sound and action of your most positive emotional experiences!

Whenever Jim, a racing car driver wants to feel fully focused, exhilarated, skilful and totally confident, he mentally places himself on the racing track and imagines himself speeding around the corners.

10. Laughter

Do you surround yourself with people and things that make you laugh? Comedy recordings, audio cassettes, videos, television, film and live performances will stimulate your humour and keep you laughing. Think about what makes you laugh and all the times you have laughed. Meditate often on the word 'laughter', involve yourself in fun activities and you will bring abundant laughter into your life.

11. Verbalise your emotions to other Optimal Thinkers

Talking rationally about, for example, your fear or anger (instead of displaying it), tends to demonstrate self-confidence and self-control. You put Optimal Thinking in charge when you say: 'This is how I feel about the problem. What's your most positive input on how to deal with it?' When you honour your feelings and apply Optimal Thinking to make the best of them and assess what is in your best interests before taking action, you demonstrate Optimal rational behaviour.

12. Do your best

W. H. Sheldon said, 'Happiness is essentially a state of going somewhere wholeheartedly.' Commit yourself to making the most of every second! Make this day the best day of your life! Attempt, as much as possible, to do your best in what you most want to do. When you continue to do your best in all circumstances, you will feel your best!

CHAPTER SIX

OPTIMAL COMMUNICATION

What's best for you?
What's best for you?
So what's best for us is...
Two Optimal Communicators

WHAT IS OPTIMAL COMMUNICATION?

Do you accept others as they are? Do you appeal to their best interests when communicating with them? Do you bring out the best in them?

All of us have experienced the frustrations of ineffective communication. You have, I'm sure, participated in conversations where one party gained at the other's expense. You have felt manipulated in some of your communications. You may have even manipulated others. You have shared your heart, only to discover the other person didn't care. Divorces, broken hearts, unsatisfying careers and broken dreams, can all result from ineffective attempts to relate to others.

Much has been written recently about effective communication which some communication experts have called 'win-win communication'. This happens when those involved take each other's goals into account and negotiate for mutual gain. This form of communication results in benefit for everyone involved, but is not necessarily Optimal.

The best means of satisfying the best interests of all concerned must be employed for Optimal communication to take place. When an Optimal purpose is shared and the best ways to achieve it sought, communicated and applied, Optimal communication flourishes. All involved are inspired to be, do and feel their best.

Do you take time to discover others' most important needs and wants? Are you in touch with their feelings, thoughts and motives? Only when we understand each other, can we determine the best ways to give each other what we need and want.

Larry, an insurance broker, did everything in his power to satisfy his clients. He aligned himself with the best products and provided superior service. When Janice bought a new car, Larry keenly evaluated the most suitable policy for her. He asked Janice numerous questions to work out her most important priorities. When Larry selected the policy best suited to Janice's needs, he explained why it was better than all the others. He encouraged her feedback, listening attentively to make sure they understood each other completely. Janice's friend Bruce, had just bought a new car and Janice enthusiastically referred him to Larry. Larry and Janice received Optimal benefit from their communication because they had each other's best interests at heart. Mutual understanding was achieved through an open exchange of information. Optimal questions were used to obtain the Optimal outcome.

An Optimal relationship provides a safe environment for all thoughts and feelings to be shared. Optimal communication involves an acceptance of all messages being delivered. The

dignity, rights, vulnerability and best interests of all parties are respected at all times.

Mary and Annette had shared a rewarding friendship for nearly eighteen years. They had met when they were both at college. They confided their deepest concerns and shared their joys on a daily basis. Annette had married and involved herself with post-graduate studies. Mary had become a public figure and was still single. Their relationship blossomed despite their changed circumstances because they continued to trust, respect and communicate openly with each other. Mary thought, 'No matter what I share with Annette, she is always on my side. She always accepts me.'

We optimise our self-image when we inspire wholehearted trust and co-operation from others. Optimal communication enables us to make the most of our relationships. Getting along as best we can with people is the key to success at home, with friends and in the business arena.

When you relate to others do you employ Optimal communication skills?

1. Do you give your undivided attention?

By giving your complete and undivided attention you show respect for the other person.

2. Do you show total interest in the other person?

William James, the psychologist, observed, 'The minute anything becomes personal with anyone, it becomes the most interesting thing in the world.' Show your interest in the other person's favourite subject: themselves.

3. Do you inspire Optimal mutual understanding?

This requires complete openness of expression. A sage said, 'Don't judge others until you have walked a mile in their moccasins.' No matter how painful the message, accept the other person's right to communicate their reality. Be aware of the main purpose of your communication and look for common ground. Discover what is most important to them and what motivates them to do their best. Think and talk in terms of their best interests.

4. Do you inspire Optimal action/resolution?

Assist the other person to make full use of their strengths and determine the Optimal action steps necessary to obtain the best outcome. Be sure to ask the best questions and listen for the best answers.

LISTENING FOR OPTIMAL COMMUNICATION

Shakespeare said, 'Give every man thine ear but few thy voice.' When you listen with not only the ear and the mind, but with the eye and the heart, you gain the understanding necessary to motivate Optimal action.

Did you know that the average person speaks at a speed of approximately 125 words per minute? And you probably think at a rate of 400 to 600 words a minute. You have listener's 'leisure' time at your disposal during every conversation. Are you interested in learning how to make the best use of it?

Here are some suggestions.

1. Give your undivided attention

Choose an environment free of distractions or cut them down to a minimum. Use a *'Do not disturb'* sign and either take the phone off the hook or hold all telephone calls. Show total involvement on your part. Lean forward, face the other person and maintain eye contact. Use the person's name early in the conversation and when prudent. Smile and nod when appropriate, let go of all judgement, be open and empathic. Show the other person you care. Be warm and understanding. Respect the other person's right to their views and feelings, particularly when they differ from yours.

2. Tune in completely to the other person's needs and wants

You can help the other person to open up by saying, 'You seem worried about something. Do you want to discuss it?' Open-ended questions will encourage the other person to talk. Avoid questions which encourage only 'yes' or 'no' answers. Use of the questions: 'who?' 'what?' 'when?' 'where?' 'how?' and 'why?' will stimulate further communication.

When you pause before responding, you are able to give

Optimal consideration to the other person's input. The pause indicates to the speaker that you are truly listening. It also encourages the other person to express all their needs and wants before you respond. This will enable you to discover how they perceive their reality.

Optimal use of comments like: 'What's on your mind?' 'Oh?' 'Tell me about that', 'Right', 'Really?', 'Yes', 'And', 'Go on', 'So?', 'Sure', will also foster further expression.

Most importantly, never interrupt! A consultant who interrupts their client won't find out what the client needs. A salesperson who listens to what their customer is saying, obtains the best information to enable them to finalise the transaction.

3. Respond with Optimal reflection

When you employ reflective listening, you restate the feeling and meaning of the communication in a way that demonstrates understanding without judgement. By rephrasing the message, and restating it to the other person, you verify that their message has been received without distortion.

You can then encourage the other person to discover their own Optimal solutions with Optimal questions like: 'What's the best thing you can do about that? What are your alternatives? Which is the best one? Why?'

Suzanne was married to a man who had great difficulty acknowledging and verbalising his feelings. During the first few years of their marriage she assisted him to identify his negative feelings by verbalising them for him without judgement. In time Simon began to acknowledge his feelings. He even learned to respect them. Suzanne nurtured emotional intimacy with him by responding with Optimal reflection.

Here's how she did it.

SIMON (annoyed): My appointment was cancelled.

SUZANNE: Oh, you must be annoyed. What's the best thing you can do about it?

SIMON (embarrassed and disappointed): I told everyone in the office that I'd win the trophy this year, and I didn't.

SUZANNE: I know it's disappointing and embarrassing, but what's the best way of handling this?

Anne and John had dated for two months. He was attracted to her, but when she shared anything painful with him, he pushed her away. Anne felt hurt and rejected. After a two week break, John contacted her again. They agreed to meet for lunch at a restaurant near Anne's office.

The chemistry between them was strong. Their conversation sparkled with mutual interest and clever humour. Anne asserted herself and John responded with Optimal reflection.

Here's a snippet of their conversation.

ANNE: John, I'm feeling a lot of different things about you. Would it be all right if we talked about them?

JOHN: Sure. Go ahead.

ANNE: I feel very hurt when I try to talk to you about something that's bothering me and you ignore my feelings. I feel like you're not accepting me for who I really am.

JOHN: Oh. I didn't know you felt upset and rejected.

ANNE: Well I do, and talking about it is hard because I don't want to feel hurt again.

JOHN: I'd like to talk about it. I understand that you're afraid I won't be sensitive because I haven't been in the past.

ANNE: Yes. I need more emotional support in a relationship through good and bad times.

JOHN: I want to be there for you whenever you need me. What's the best thing I can do to be more sensitive to your feelings?

It is often best to reflect your understanding of the meaning of the message being delivered. It may be necessary to recap significant parts of a lengthy conversation to ensure you have understood the other person correctly. To promote Optimal feedback you can say: 'Is that what you mean?' or 'Did I understand you correctly?'

Optimal listeners listen reflectively without judgement to gain understanding. They then ask Optimal questions to assist others to discover their own Optimal solutions.

NON-VERBAL COMMUNICATION

Did you know that approximately 85 per cent of our communication is non-verbal? Non-verbal messages are hailed by our communication experts as the best means of communicating emotions. Non-verbal messages not only reveal feelings, but also show how the person is relating to those feelings. When verbal and non-verbal messages contradict each other, it is best to rely on the non-verbal message.

James, a gentle employer, was careful not to hurt others' feelings. The financial controller, Carol, had just completed an internal audit, discovering many problems in the process. She discussed her findings with James. Wearing a worried facial expression, James told Carol he was pleased with the results. Carol noticed the discrepancy between James's verbal and non-verbal response.

Let's tune in on the rest of their conversation:

CAROL: James, you mentioned you're pleased with the results, but you don't look very happy. How do you really feel about it?

JAMES: Carol, I believe you did an excellent job with the audit, but I am a little worried about the losses we have incurred because of the duplication of invoices.

CAROL: Yes, I know it's a problem. What is the best system we can implement to stop it happening?

Bill wanted to buy a car but didn't know how to go about getting the best deal. Frank, a car mechanic and friend, was happy to help. They decided that he would get the best buy through a private owner.

The first car they saw had everything going for it. It looked terrific, the colour was perfect, the price was right and it drove like a dream. Frank asked the owner if the car had been well serviced. The owner defensively folded his arms across his chest, and said yes. Frank then asked if the car had been in an accident. The owner, displaying the same defensive posture, declared that it had not been in an accident. He did not look Frank in the eye. Frank knew how to read non-verbal messages in clusters and in context. He could see from the owner's responses that the car had been in an accident. Noticing the incongruent non-verbal messages, Frank asked if he could see the service records. The owner said he had misplaced them. Frank and Bill left without the car!

The next car they saw also looked great and was in the right price range. The owner talked enthusiastically about how well he had maintained it, and proudly showed Bill and Frank the service manual. The service record couldn't have been better. As the owner discussed the car, he displayed completely open body language. He looked Bill and Frank straight in the eye and leaned forward throughout the conversation. Frank and Bill drove the car around the block, Frank checked it over mechanically, and after a short discussion, Bill told the owner he had a deal.

Body language
Body language experts have discovered that there are certain gestures that signal quite distinct messages. See if you recognise the messages that these gestures can often signal.

Facial expressions, postures and gestures
Lifting one eyebrow . . . . . disbelief

Rubbing nose . . . . . doubt, rejection, negation

Rubbing eye . . . . . don't want to see

Winking . . . . . intimacy

Hand across mouth when talking . . . . . lying

Head to side . . . . . interested

Head erect . . . . . not so interested

Head in palm of hand . . . . . boredom

Stroking chin . . . . . evaluating

Open hands . . . . . friendliness, honesty, sincerity

Arms folded across chest with closed fists . . . . . defensive

Leaning closer to someone . . . . . more interested

Leaning away from someone . . . . . less interested

Legs crossed, swinging foot back and forward . . . . . impatience

Shrugging shoulders . . . . . indifference

Tapping fingers . . . . . impatience

Sitting with one leg over chair . . . . . lack of co-operation

Hands on hips . . . . . aggressive

Cleaning glasses . . . . . delaying procedure

Rounded shoulders, looking down . . . . . pessimistic, lacking confidence

Standing straight, looking ahead . . . . . confident

Leaning back with both hands supporting head . . . . . superiority

Rubbing hands . . . . . expectation, excitement

The mirroring of gestures

Have you ever observed that when people like each other, they often mirror each other's gestures? The unconscious message of 'this person's like me' is relayed through duplication of their non-verbal behaviour.

When you want to optimise rapport with someone, start by subtly mirroring their non-verbal messages. You can then attempt to lead non-verbally. If the other person follows, you have been given permission to lead. If not, simply return to mirroring the other person's message.

John Hawthorne, a highly successful corporate president, excelled in duplicating the breathing, postures, gestures and tone of voice of others. Within a few minutes he could create a strong bond and rapport with people he had never met.

Upon learning of John Hawthorne's method, Michael, a facsimile salesman, decided to try it out. He had been negotiating the sale of the latest facsimile machine with Maxine, an unpublished writer, for several weeks. She was giving him mixed messages, sometimes as though she wanted to buy, other times as though she didn't, and he didn't know how to interpret them. He couldn't understand exactly why he hadn't been able to finalise the transaction.

Michael decided to mirror her non-verbal behaviour to try and gain rapport with her. As she moved from posture to posture he gently duplicated her gestures. He started to experience her discomfort. He realised that Maxine feared the consequences of an extravagant purchase. Michael then was sufficiently sensitive to suggest a less expensive model. He soothed her anxiety as he continued to mirror her gestures. Maxine began to relax. She sensed that Michael was on her side and decided to invest in the less expensive machine. By mirroring her non-verbal behaviour Michael gained the understanding he required to satisfy her best interests.

For each of the following illustrations decide what emotion or message is being communicated and what would be the best way to respond.

Eye movements

Much has been said recently about reading eye movements. Those involved with neuro-linguistic programming study how verbal and non-verbal communication affect our nervous system and behaviour. They tell us:

When our eyes move upward, we are visualising — creating pictures in our mind.

When we look straight across to the left or right, or downwards to the left, we are in the audio or listening state — creating sounds or listening to them.

When we look downwards to the right, we are in the kinaesthetic state, which includes bodily sensations, feelings and emotions.

It has been noted that when we are visualising the future, we generally look to our dominant side, that is, the side of our dominant hand. When we are accessing our memory, we look to our non-dominant side.

For most right-handed people:

Looking to the left indicates an emphasis on past recall.

Looking to the right indicates an emphasis on the future.

Below are some questions which will elicit the specific eye movements mentioned previously:

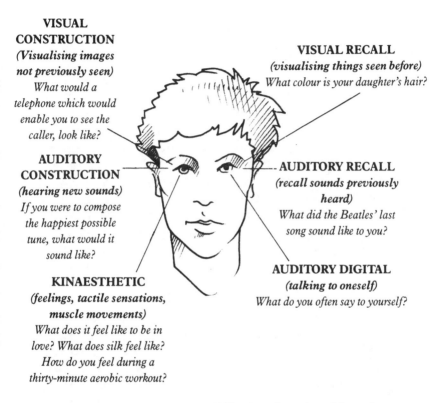

VISUAL CONSTRUCTION
(Visualising images not previously seen)
What would a telephone which would enable you to see the caller, look like?

VISUAL RECALL
(visualising things seen before)
What colour is your daughter's hair?

AUDITORY CONSTRUCTION
(hearing new sounds)
If you were to compose the happiest possible tune, what would it sound like?

AUDITORY RECALL
(recall sounds previously heard)
What did the Beatles' last song sound like to you?

KINAESTHETIC
(feelings, tactile sensations, muscle movements)
What does it feel like to be in love? What does silk feel like? How do you feel during a thirty-minute aerobic workout?

AUDITORY DIGITAL
(talking to oneself)
What do you often say to yourself?

Right-handed people who have difficulty picturing things from the past can look up to the left to jog their memory. When rehearsing a speech, they can look across to their right ear to hear how it will sound.

For those who are left-handed:

Looking to the left indicates an emphasis on the future.

Looking to the right indicates an emphasis on the past.

By watching the other person's eye movements, you can discover which mode (visual, audio or kinaesthetic) they predominantly use to relate to the world around them and adjust your communication to suit.

OPTIMAL VERBAL COMMUNICATION

Man's supreme achievement in the world is communication from personality to personality.
Karl Jaspers, philosopher

When you use Optimal words such as best, favourite, greatest, highest, top, and mastery, and those that express your primary mode of thinking, either visual, auditory or kineasthetic, you are communicating at your best and encouraging others to be their best. You experience the enjoyment of being your best together.

You can use different words for different people depending on what their major thought processes are like. When speaking with people who function primarily in the visual mode, such as decorators, fashion designers and artists, it is best to use visual language. For example: 'Let me show you the best way to do this.' 'Do you want to take a look at the top of the range model?' 'I see exactly what you mean.' 'Can you picture the best outcome?' Paint vivid and specific pictures with Optimal words.

When speaking with those who function primarily in the audio mode, such as sound engineers, musicians or singers, it is best to use audio terminology. Some examples are: 'Does that sound right to you?' 'It rings true to me', and 'Tell me about your best product.'

You will communicate best with those who perceive their reality primarily through their feelings, using kinaesthetic or feeling words, such as 'How do you feel about this?' 'I have a gut feeling this is going to be the best job I've ever had', or 'Are you completely comfortable with that?'

Optimal verbal assertion

With Optimal verbal assertion, you state all that occurs at the time. You share how you feel, what you think, what you want and don't want.

The passage below decribes a person who approaches life with Optimal assertion. Underline which aspects you presently identify with and circle those you would like to adopt. This will make you aware of where you stand now in relation to where you want to be.

I take complete responsibility for my life. I accept and respect myself. I respect my right to live my life as I choose and to do the best I can. I make sure that my personal needs are met and I experience appropriate amounts of fear, anger, trust, joy and love. My values are worthy of my own appreciation.

I communicate openly and honestly. I communicate my feelings and thoughts when doing so is in my best interests. I know the best way to assert my needs and I am comfortable with the use of 'I' statements, such as 'I feel' and 'I want'. I seek the co-operation of others with statements like, 'Let's do this' or 'Can we have your best price?' I ask Optimal questions to obtain the best answers. I respect the dignity and rights of others and I support their best interests as much as possible.

I am empathic and use such statements as 'How do you feel about this?' and 'What do you see in this?' I confront others honestly and directly, stating all that occurs, as it occurs. I do not allow others to violate my rights or take advantage of me.

How do you react when threatened? When you feel threatened or your rights are violated, communicating your response will create understanding. Often people are unaware that they are violating your rights until you let them know. They are here to live their life as best they can. When you verbalise the problem specifically, as it occurs, and immediately negotiate the best solution, you are free to get on with your SUPREME goals, without suppressing feelings of anger and hurt. The goal of Optimal verbal assertion when confronting unwanted behaviour, is to provide the best verbal stimulus to stop the intrusive behaviour. This is done using a three-part statement, consisting of a non-judgemental depiction of the undesirable behaviour, the feelings experienced, and then the effects of the behaviour. The three-part statement is immediately followed by an Optimal question to evoke the Optimal solution.

Robert was annoyed because he was continually cleaning up after Betty. He asserted: 'When you leave your papers and clothes in the living room [non-judgemental depiction of unwanted behaviour], I feel very annoyed [feelings], because it makes more work for me to keep the room tidy [effects of behaviour]. What can we do to get the best solution for both of us [Optimal question]?'

Regina felt disappointed and angry when her friend called to cancel their meeting at the last minute. Regina responded with Optimal assertion when she said: 'When you cancel our meetings at the last minute, I feel frustrated because it affects my plans for the rest of the day. What's the best thing we can do to make sure we give each other plenty of notice from now on?'

Don was trying to study for his exams. When his wife's friends played cards at home Don couldn't concentrate. There was too much noise. Don became particularly angry when his wife talked loudly. He confronted her with: 'When you make a lot of noise while I'm trying to study, I feel angry because it makes it difficult for me to concentrate on my work. What's the best solution for both of us?'

Allan, a partner in a large accounting firm, was a poor manager. He openly belittled his employees at the weekly staff meetings and also demonstrated his contempt for them by swearing at them. Nanette employed Optimal verbal assertion when she said: 'Allan, when you use inappropriate language in my presence, I feel uncomfortable, because I don't feel respected. How can we best solve this problem?'

Do you currently feel annoyed by someone's behaviour? The next time the person displays that behaviour, tell them how you feel without judging them. Request the other person's input in finding the best solution.

When time is short, you can respond quickly to put-downs with statements like: 'Why is that so important to you?', 'What do you mean by that?' or 'Was that a put-down?' Always follow up with an Optimal question such as: 'What's the best way to resolve this?', 'What is your most constructive feedback?' or 'In your opinion, what's the best solution for all concerned?'

OPTIMAL CONFLICT RESOLUTION

Do you avoid conflict because you fear the unpleasantness involved in facing it? Understanding and communication are optimised when you acknowledge and deal most effectively with conflict. Crises are avoided and Optimal decision making can take place. Sometimes the presence of conflict is destructive and impedes progress. At other times, it doesn't. When there is complete absence of conflict, often the need for change is denied, hidden resentments accumulate, problems aren't dealt with and creativity is retarded.

When you resolve conflicts with Optimal communication, the best interests of all are considered and the best solution negotiated. You are best equipped to make the most of differences when you fully integrate and employ Optimal conflict resolution skills. *To resolve a conflict, willingness by all those involved is essential.*

Consider a conflict situation between a father and son. The son's needs are not met or even considered. The father just reminds the son who's boss by imposing his solution on the son. A fearful, resentful son submits to the father's domination. This is a win-lose resolution.

On some occasions, where the son offers the solution to the father, the father's needs aren't met. The father begins to feel fearful that he has allowed his son to get 'one-up' on him. He fears his son's loss of respect. Again win-lose conflict resolution occurs.

OPTIMAL AFFIRMATIONS

**When I ask the best questions
I obtain the best answers.**

▼

I ask for what I want.

▼

**I mirror others' non-verbal
gestures to enjoy Optimal
rapport with them.**

▼

**When others speak to me I
give them my full attention.**

▼

**I ask Optimal questions to
assist others to discover their
own Optimal solutions.**

I communicate the best means of satisfying the best interests of all concerned.

▼

I communicate with Optimal assertion.

▼

I always restate the other person's message to make sure that I have understood it correctly.

▼

I always respect the dignity, rights and feelings of others.

Some ways of imposing this win-lose form of conflict resolution are:

- Ordering, directing: 'Do it this way.'
- Judging: 'You're wrong.'
- Distracting: 'You think you've got worries, let me tell you about mine.'
- Reassuring: 'It will work out fine in the end.'
- Warning: 'If you do that again, I'll fire you.'
- Praising: 'You're good at this but...'

These approaches inhibit communication and, as a result, impede conflict resolution.

The objective of the two-way Optimal conflict resolution process is to find the best solution for all concerned. Only those involved in the conflict partake in its resolution. In Optimal conflict resolution discussions, it is imperative that respect for others' self-esteem is always displayed. Concentrate fully on the issue, listen with Optimal reflection and organise the best follow-up date.

The following seven step formula can be used whenever you seek the best solution to your problems and conflicts.

Step 1. Clearly define the problem/conflict.

Step 2. Define the main purpose of the solution.
Why do I need the solution?

Step 3. Decide on all the information needed.
You may already have all the necessary information or you may need to gather additional information.

Step 4. Generate possible solutions.
Brainstorm. Do not judge solutions at this stage.

Step 5. Evaluate possible solutions in light of the information collected.
View the pros and cons and evaluate the consequences.

Step 6. Decide upon and implement the best solution.
What? who? where? why? how? when's the best time?

Step 7. Choose the Optimal follow-up date.

HOW WELL DO YOU COMMUNICATE?

Below are several statements to help you gain understanding about your current skills in communication. In each sentence, there is space allotted to add one of the following words: always, often, usually, sometimes, rarely, never.

For each statement decide the best possible action you can take to improve your communication with others.

1. I . . . . give my complete attention to others when they talk to me.

2. I . . . . maintain eye contact throughout the conversation.

3. I . . . . show empathy.

4. I . . . . encourage others to talk.

5. I . . . . ask Optimal questions to assist others to discover their own Optimal solutions.

6. I . . . . do all I can to gain complete understanding of the other person's most important needs, wants and expectations.

7. I . . . . ask for clarification of whatever I don't fully understand.

8. I . . . . paraphrase the other person's message to make sure that I have understood it correctly.

9. I . . . . experience pleasant exchanges in my personal life (with spouse, children, friends).

10. I . . . . experience pleasant encounters with employees and fellow workers.

11. I . . . . experience at least one satisfying encounter with people who are important to me every day.

12. When I communicate with people I . . . . accept them. I do not judge them.

13. When communicating with others I . . . . read their non-verbal language.

14. I . . . . bring out the best in others.

If your response to any statement was:
Always, your attitude and skills are Optimal — congratulations!

Often or *usually,* your attitude and skills are extraordinary, close to Optimal. It will be easy for you to bridge the gap.

Sometimes, your attitude and skills are mediocre. Are you ready to take action to rectify this?

Rarely or *never,* this is a negative area for you. Are you willing and ready to take steps to rectify this right now? You do deserve to have exactly what you want!

OBSTACLES TO OPTIMAL COMMUNICATION

All of us experience barriers in our communication with others. A large barrier to Optimal communication is lack of awareness of your own feelings, beliefs and expectations. When you don't understand yourself, it is difficult to understand others. You may also feel uncomfortable because of an inadequate vocabulary or poor skills in transmitting Optimal messages. You may use an excessive number of words to communicate your ideas. Perhaps you have psychological problems. You may be suffering from emotional stress, or a stress related disease. You may feel handicapped by physiological impediments, such as poor eyesight or poor hearing. Do you have difficulty with mixed messages? Are your non-verbal and verbal messages consistent? When you exhibit non-verbal messages such as slumping over, preoccupation with something else or no eye contact, you set up barriers to Optimal communication.

Judging others, whether positively or negatively, inhibits Optimal communication. Offering your own solutions to others is a means of attempting to control them and doesn't show respect for the other person's ability to find their own Optimal solutions. When you avoid the other person's concerns by diverting the conversation you also inhibit the process of Optimal communication.

Many people have overcome enormous barriers in order to communicate their message to others. Franklin D. Roosevelt inspired strength and heroism to an entire nation from his wheelchair. Winston Churchill suffered from a severe speech impediment into early adulthood. Helen Keller inspired courage and hope even though she was blind and deaf. You can do it too!

CHAPTER SEVEN

OPTIMAL LEADERSHIP

> The best soldier does not attack.
> The superior fighter succeeds without violence.
> The greatest conqueror wins without a struggle.
> The most successful manager leads without dictating.
> This is called intelligent nonaggressiveness.
> This is called mastery of men.
> **LAO-TSU, Tao Teh King**

OPTIMAL LEADERS AND OPTIMAL VISIONS

You have, I'm sure, been part of a group or team at some time in your life. You grew up in a family, played in a sporting team, joined a social club, and have worked with others. Chances are, you are involved with more than one group of people, professionally, socially or otherwise, right now.

Do you attract the best people to help you achieve what you want? Do you help others find the best ways to obtain what they want? Do others do their best, and achieve what they want, by helping you realise your Optimal purpose?

The best leaders are Optimal Thinkers who are wholeheartedly committed to their Optimal purpose. Their vision or purpose is an expression of what they most deeply care about. They dedicate their lives to what is most meaningful to them. Sometimes their vision can take years or even a lifetime to manifest. In their vision, they sweep past the ordinary and extraordinary, into the world of the Optimal.

Martin Luther King had a vision of equal opportunity for all races. His vision expressed his deep personal commitment to acknowledging God's presence within every human being. For him, God's presence unified all of mankind. This knowledge inspired him to share his vision of racial equality.

Lee Iaccoca shared his Optimal vision, when he said, 'Chrysler won't be the biggest, just the best'. In Optimal corporations, the mission statement articulates the organisation's most desirable direction, and what the organisation must care about most to achieve this vision.

Here is part of an Optimal corporate mission statement:

The highest calibre leaders, managers and employees
fully committed
to providing
the highest quality service
the most competitive fees
and the best leadership
in the financial planning field
world-wide.
Satisfying our customers' needs
is our best opportunity.

Optimal corporate mission statements usually include Optimal objectives, approach to customer needs, management philosophy and ethical standards. Financial goals and employee commitment are often mentioned.

The best leaders demonstrate complete commitment to their mission. They love and treasure their vision enough to do all they can to manifest it in reality. They see its implementation as an opportunity to make the best use of their own talents, abilities and energies. They are true to themselves and others. These people point the best way forward. A sage once said, 'The first test of a leader is that he leaves behind in others the conviction and will to carry on'. Optimal leaders galvanise others to involve themselves wholeheartedly because it is in their best interests to do so.

These leaders often illustrate their vision with compelling stories. Henry Ford inspired the full co-operation of his people through his stories. He'd never say, 'I want this done!' He'd say, 'I wonder if we can do it'. Many Optimal leaders encourage input from their people. The collective vision is one to which leaders and their people can fully commit their best efforts.

Think carefully about the most important group with which you are presently involved. It may be your family, your company or a sporting organisation. What is its Optimal purpose? Which of the following methods were used to clarify its purpose?

1. Leader shared the Optimal purpose, which the people accepted.

2. Leader shared the Optimal purpose to gain acceptance.

3. Leader presented the Optimal purpose and responded to questions.

4. Leader presented a tentative Optimal purpose, subject to changes, after input from everyone else.

5. Leader presented a direction, obtained input, then formulated the Optimal purpose.

6. Leader defined the parameters within which the team formulated the Optimal purpose.

7. Leader and team jointly created the Optimal purpose.

Jim, a football coach, presented his Optimal vision to the players, asked for their input, and responded to their questions. After much discussion, they were all convinced their Optimal mission was simply to become the best team in the league.

Studies have shown that the best leaders focus on both the task and their people. They include their people in the planning and decision making processes. Japanese leaders, for example, involve numerous people from many different levels of their organisations in decision making.

At Findhorn, a decentralised and democratic organisation in Scotland, 'focalisers' assist in the decision making process with their group. The focalisers serve to focus, rather than direct, the individuals within the group. When a new innovation is explored, a team member opens up the conversation, inviting the others to share their viewpoints. Agreement is finally obtained through the alignment of individual input and the group purpose.

OPTIMAL LEADERS AND REALITY

The best leaders interact with their people to bring the Optimal vision into reality. They are not lone rangers. They do not lead as 'saviours', encouraging passive following. Optimal leaders do not seek to usurp others' power and responsibility.

Parents, prime ministers and presidents act for, and in the best interests of, their children and nations. Chief executive officers act in the best interests of their stockholders and employees. A young blind woman recently acted as spokesperson for the blind on a national television show. Her sensitive disclosure of their needs and difficulties moved a record number of viewers to render assistance. Speaking for, and acting in the best interests of others, requires cohesiveness and is most effectively done when leaders see themselves as members of their group.

Do you accurately assess your current reality? Optimal leaders plan the best use of available resources and evaluate their greatest strengths, weaknesses, opportunities and threats. They determine what is most relevant to the achievement of their mission, and launch their vision with their feet on the ground. Achievable goals and Optimal conditions are designed to motivate their people to do their best. Methods of operation are arranged so that their people can achieve their own goals, by directing their best efforts toward the organisational objectives. Performance is monitored and measured against Optimal achievable standards.

These leaders enlist the best efforts of the best people to fulfil their mission. They seek wholehearted commitment from those whose skills and expertise are most suited for the various tasks required. Manageable tasks are assigned to the most appropriate members. Clear responsibilities and structures are defined, so collective effort is optimised. Optimal leaders know what motivates each person to do their best, and work with these motivations to achieve Optimal standards and objectives.

Geraldine, a former business consultant, joined a well-known insurance company after passing the entrance tests. Her most important goals were found to be compatible with the corporate mission, a prerequisite for her acceptance into the corporation. Walter, an Optimal leader, had structured a schedule which inspired Geraldine's total commitment. Together they decided upon an achievable sales target to ensure her best efforts during her first year. They also worked out what she had to do on a daily and weekly basis to attain her SUPREME goal.

Geraldine was happy with the conditions of her employment. The office environment encouraged her to concentrate fully on her work. Every morning she attended mandatory meetings where she learned the most important ingredients for success from the top achievers. She had to complete SUPREME assignments such as calling ten new people, or mastering knowledge of a specific product, on a daily basis. She measured her progress by filling out weekly reports.

Walter kept track of Geraldine's performance and his feedback always motivated her to do her best work. When she achieved target, he acknowledged her success, both personally and publicly. When she surpassed her previous best efforts, they celebrated!

Are you willing to assess the current reality and direction of the group which is most important to you? In your notebook now, answer the following questions:

Why does your group or team exist?

What is its Optimal purpose?

What are the most important objectives of your group this year?

What is the best way to achieve them within specific time frames?

What are the group's greatest strengths?

What are its major weaknesses?

What are you doing to optimise the strengths of your group?

What are you doing to minimise its weaknesses?

What are the major opportunities available to your group this year?

What are the major threats to your group this year?

What are the strengths of the individuals in your group?

Does their task/job profile fully utilise their strengths?

How is your group's mission helping you to achieve your own Optimal purpose?

MOTIVATING OTHERS TO DO THEIR BEST

Do you show appreciation for others as they are, and assist them to make the most of themselves? The best leaders begin by understanding their people's needs and desires. These leaders discover what their people value most, and what beliefs and causes they are committed to. They help them decide what they want, and support them in taking the best steps to achieve it. They encourage their people to make the most of their strengths and accomplishments. They know their success lies in their ability to work with others to function at their best. *Optimal leaders believe there is no better occupation than to inspire another to be their best.*

These leaders often share success stories to inspire Optimal performance. When their people experience a slump, they

OPTIMAL AFFIRMATIONS

I attract the best people.

▼

I always listen reflectively without judgement to gain complete understanding.

▼

I bring out the best in others.

▼

What I do brings out the best in you.

▼

Everyone is doing their best.

▼

We are all doing our best.

▼

I help others recognise their ability to create what's best for them.

The greatest gift I can give others is the example of my own life working.

▼

Everybody co-operates with me.

▼

It's the best thing for all of us.

▼

I always think of what is best for everyone.

▼

People usually do the best they can under the circumstances.

▼

Everyone and everything is of Optimal benefit to me.

remind them of their successes. They talk about others' struggles, conflicts, persistence, and eventual triumphs.

Tom, a real estate developer, was devastated when he lost all his money during a recession. He borrowed enough money to start again, and eventually became one of the largest developers in the country. Tom was a compassionate man who cared about his people. He took time to get to know and understand them and always encouraged their best efforts. Graham, his site manager of seven years, had been irritable lately and had made some serious mistakes. When Tom asked Graham what was bothering him, Graham told him that he had recently lost all of his savings in the stock market. He didn't have enough money to pay for his children's school fees and there were other bills he couldn't cover. Tom immediately advanced Graham the money he needed, and organised additional work for him on the weekends. He shared what it was like when he had lost his money, and what it had taken to bounce back. He talked about others who had triumphed over even more difficult circumstances. He then reminded Graham of all his accomplishments over the past seven years. He showed full confidence in him. Graham dedicated his best efforts to the organisation and, in time, recouped his financial losses.

Optimal leaders do not manipulate others by trying to persuade them to do what is not in their best interests. They relate to others solely in terms of their best interests.

Michael, the president of the local yachting club, had counted on Henry's administrative assistance for almost ten years. Henry was now studying to complete his master's degree and was often up until the early hours of the morning. He was feeling guilty because he hardly spent any time with his family. Michael was concerned that Henry had overcommitted himself and enouraged him to evaluate his priorities. Henry admitted that the club's administrative activities had become a burden and asked Michael to find someone else to handle some of his responsibilities. Michael agreed and immediately secured the best available administrative assistance.

The best leaders are Optimal communicators. They are skilled at convincing others of the value of their ideas and can communicate with people on their terms. They understand non-verbal communication and make the most of it. Optimal leaders employ Optimal verbal assertion and listening skills. They encourage their people to express themselves fully. Many leaders believe, 'If I say it, they can doubt me; if they say it, it's true'. Optimal leaders are sensitive to the needs and expectations of their people and seek regular, honest feedback from them. They always encourage respect and understanding within their team.

Recently I conducted an Optimal leadership seminar with top management in a rapidly expanding organisation. I was

delighted when the leader declared that regardless of position or length of service, everyone was to be treated with equal respect. He repeatedly said, 'Treat others as you would like to be treated'.

During his presidency, Ronald Reagan displayed a plaque which said, 'You can go everywhere in life, when you give others the credit'. The best leaders acknowledge their people for their contributions. They are very specific with praise. They say, 'You've done a fantastic job with this report', or 'I am grateful that I can count on you to be punctual'. They value their people for being themselves. They also recognise and applaud achievement, and celebrate success when it occurs. You can acknowledge and celebrate the achievements of your people with letters of appreciation, weekend getaways, dinners, flowers, award ceremonies, plaques, gifts, cash awards, a handshake, a smile and applause. Many Optimal leaders claim they have the finest jobs in the world because they invest much of their time honouring other people.

Are you skilled in the art of reprimanding others? Do you confirm facts and identify undesirable behaviour specifically? The best leaders act immediately to correct unwanted behaviour. They do not criticise others' motives, but direct their comments to the behaviour, not the person. When Optimal leaders have to criticise, they sometimes do it in the form of a question. This is always followed by another Optimal question to obtain the best solution. Optimal leaders show their feelings of anger, annoyance and frustration when appropriate. They resolve negative emotions, rather than deny them, and encourage their expression to the most appropriate person.

Mary, a youth group leader, was annoyed with a boy who continually came late to meetings. She confronted him by saying, 'When you come late to meetings, I feel annoyed because it disturbs the rest of us. Can you tell me why you have been coming late?' After he explained the reason for his lateness, Mary asked, 'What's the best thing you can do to make sure you are on time from now on?'

Optimal leaders discover what 'the best' means to their people, appeal to their best interests, stimulate in them the desire to be their best and then acknowledge them for doing their best. They are easily recognised because somehow their people always achieve the best results. When the Optimal leader's work is complete, their people often say, 'We did it ourselves!'

CHARACTERISTICS OF OPTIMAL LEADERS

Aristotle said, 'Character is the most effective agent of persuasion'. Optimal leaders display character in their voices, manners, postures, actions, mannerisms and facial expressions. They follow through on what they say they will do. They honour agreements, and demonstrate consistency and commitment. They act with integrity and inspire trust. They look for the best ways things can be done and use humour judiciously.

Do you accept mistakes, take the best actions to correct them, learn from them and move on? The best leaders understand that failure, and taking risks, are part of success. They have the courage to fail amidst their successes. Theodore Roosevelt said, 'The only man who never makes a mistake is the man who never does anything'.

How do you react to change? The best leaders make the most of it. They welcome change, adapt to it, and learn from it. They always encourage innovative action, flexibility and Optimal feedback, and support their people's collaborative efforts. The best leaders promote initiative, the generation of ideas, risk taking and autonomy. They encourage their people to be creative and independent with problem solving. One Optimal school principal tells his staff. 'Do everything in your power to bring me the best solutions, and not problems. If you have a problem you can't solve, I'm here for you.'

Optimal leaders are also skilled at decision making, knowing that the worst decision is, generally, no decision. They keep their composure, choose the best times to make decisions, and then take the best actions.

When resolving conflict, Optimal leaders consider which alternatives will help those involved meet their needs in ways that move the organisation closest to its SUPREME goals. They consider which alternatives are most likely to reduce conflict and minimise opposition to these objectives. They also examine what must be sacrificed to achieve the best resolution.

A study by Professor Weston Agor, done in 1984, showed that intuitive leaders are most likely to be found at the top of organisations. Do you acknowledge your intuition? Optimal leaders allow their intuition and Optimal Thinking to work hand-in-hand.

The best leaders often lack many resources we take for granted. Blind and deaf Helen Keller inspired the world with her thinking and accomplishments. She demonstrated that a full life is possible for each and every one of us. When she received her honorary law degree at the University of Glasgow, she responded with, 'It is a sign, Sir, that silence and darkness need not block progress of the immortal human spirit'.

Your Optimal Voice is available in silence, darkness, sunshine and song. Where is it leading you?

For more information about seminars and products on Optimal Thinking, contact:

The World Academy of Personal Development Inc.
449 S. Beverly Drive, Suite 214, Beverly Hills, CA 90212
Tel: (310) 557-2761 Fax: (310) 557-2762
info@optimalthinking.com
www.optimalthinking.com

BIBLIOGRAPHY

Adams, John D., Ph.D., *Transforming Leadership: From Vision to Results*, Miles River Press, Virginia, 1986

Bach, Richard, *Jonathan Livingstone Seagull*, The Macmillan Company, New York, 1970

Badaracco, Josheph L. and Ellsworth, Richard R., *Leadership and the Quest For Integrity*, Harvard Business School Press, Boston, 1989

Bandler, Richard and Grinder, John, *Frogs into Princes*, People Press, New York, 1979

Blanchard, Kenneth, Ph.D. and Johnson, Spencer, M.D., *The One Minute Manager*, Willow Books, London, 1983

Bloomfield, Harold H., M.D. and Kory, Robert B., *Inner Joy: New Strategies for Adding More Pleasure to Your Life*, Wyden, New York, 1980

Bloomfield, Harold H., M.D. and Felder, Leonard, Ph.D., *Making Peace With Yourself*, Ballantine Books, New York, 1985

Bolton, Robert, Ph.D., *People Skills*, Simon & Schuster Australia, Sydney, 1986

Branden, Nathaniel, *How To Raise Your Self-Esteem*, Bantam Books, New York, 1987

Branden, Nathaniel, *The Psychology of Self-Esteem*, Nash, New York, 1969

Briggs, Dorothy Corkille, *Celebrate Yourself*, Doubleday, Garden City, 1977

Burns, David D., M.D., *Feeling Good, The New Mood Therapy*, William Morrow and Co., New York, 1980

Canfield, Jack, *Self Esteem and Peak Performance*, (cassette tape series), Career Track Publications, Colorado, 1987

De Angelis, Barbara, Ph.D., *How To Make Love All the Time*, Rawson Associates, New York, 1987

De Bono, Edward, *Atlas of Management Thinking*, Penguin Books

De Bono, Edward, *The Happiness Purpose*, Penguin Books, Middlesex, 1977

De Bono, Edward, *Lateral Thinking*, Penguin Books, London, 1970

De Bono, Edward, *Six Thinking Hats*, Penguin Books, London, 1985

The Diagram Group Staff, *The Brain: A Users Manual*, Putnam Publishing Group, 1987

Dyer, Wayne W., Dr, *Your Erroneous Zones*, Harper & Row, New York, 1976

Ehrenberg, Miriam and Otto, Ph.D.'s, *Optimum Brain Power: A Total Program for Increasing Your Intelligence*, Gamut Books, New York, 1987

Emery, Stewart, *Actualizations*, Dolphin Books, Doubleday and Company, Garden City, 1977

Fast, Julius, *Body Lanugauge*, M. Evans and Co. Inc., Philadelphia, 1970

Fritz, Robert, *The Path of Least Resistance*, Stillpoint Publishing Company, Massachusetts, 1984

Garfield, Charles A., Ph.D. and Bennett, Hal Zina, *Peak Performance*, Jeremy P. Tarcher Inc., Los Angeles, 1984

Gawain, Shakti, *Creative Visualization*, Whatever Publishing, Mill Valley, 1978

Gillies, Jerry, *Moneylove*, Warner Books, New York, 1978

Harrison, Allen F. and Bramson, Robert M., Ph.D., *The Art of Thinking*, The Berkely Publishing Group, New York, 1982

Hay, Louise, *You Can Heal Your Life*, Coleman Publishing, Farmingdale, New York, 1984

Heller, Robert, *The Supermanagers*, Truman Talley Books, New York, 1984

Hersey, Paul, Dr, *The Situational Leader*, Warner Books, New York, 1984

Hill, Napoleon, *Think and Grow Rich*, Elsevier-Dutton Publishing Co. Inc., 1965

Hill, Napoleon and Stone, W. Clement, *Success Through a Positive Mental Attitude*, Pocket Books, New York, 1960

Hopkins, Tom, *The Official Guide to Success Vol 1*, Tom Hopkins International, Scottsdale, Arizona, 1983

Jampolsky, Gerald, *Love Is Letting Go of Fear*, Celestial Arts, Millbrae, California, 1979

Jeffers, Susan, Ph.D., *Feel The Fear and Do It Anyway*, Harcourt Brace Jovanovich, Florida, 1987

Kassorla, Irene C., Dr, *Go For It!*, Futura Publications, London, 1984

Keyes, Ken, *Handbook to Higher Consciousness*, Living Love Publications, Marina Del Rey, California, 1980

Lakein, Alan, *How To Get Control of Your Time and Life*, New American Library, New York, 1974

Levinson, Harry and Stuart Rosenthal, CEO, *Corporate Leadership in Action*, Basic Books Inc., New York, 1984

LeCron, Leslie M., *Self Hypnotism*, Prentice-Hall Inc., Englewood Cliffs, 1964

Mackay, Harvey, *Swim With The Sharks Without Being Eaten Alive*, Ivy Books, New York, 1989

Malone, Paul B III, *Love 'Em and Lead 'Em*, Synergy Press, Annandale, Virginia, 1986

Maltz, Maxwell, *Psycho-Cybernetics*, Prentice-Hall Inc., Englewood Cliffs, 1960

Mandino, Og, *Og Mandino's University of Success*, Bantam Books, New York, 1982

Maslow, A.H., *Motivation and Personality*, Harper, New York, 1954

McGinnis, Alan Loy, *Bringing Out The Best In People*, Lutheran Publishing House, Mineapolis, 1985

McInnes, Lisa Jane, *Why Wasn't I Told?* Cassette Learning Systems, Australia, 1986

McKay, Matthew, Ph.D. and Fanning, Patrick, *Self-Esteem*, New Harbinger Publications, Oakland, 1987

McKay, Matthew, Ph.D., Davis, Martha and Fanning, Patrick, *Thoughts and Feelings: The Art of Cognitive Stress Intervention*, New Harbinger Publications, Oakland, 1981

Meyer, Paul J., *The Dynamics of Personal Leadership*, Success Motivation Inc., Texas, 1969

Meyer, Paul J., *Executive Time Management*, Success Motivation Inc., Texas, 1979

Murphy, Joseph, *The Power of Your Subconscious Mind*, Bantam Books, New York, 1963

Newman, James W., *Release Your Brakes!*, Warner Books, New York, 1977

Nirenberg, Gerald I., *The Art of Negotiating*, Hawthorn Books Inc., New York, 1968

Nirenberg, Gerald I. and Calero, Henry H., *How To Read A Person Like A Book*, Pocket Books, New York, 1971

Patent, Arnold M., *You Can Have It All*, Celebration Publishing, New York, 1984

Peter, J. Laurence, Dr and Dana, Bill, *The Laughter Prescription*, Ballantine Books, New York, 1982

Peters, Tom and Austin, Nancy, *A Passion For Excellence*, Random House, New York, 1985

Peters, Thomas J. and Waterman, Robert H., Jr, *In Search of Excellence*, Harper & Row, New York, 1982

Postle, Denis, *The Mind Gymnasium: How to Use Your Mind for Personal Growth*, Simon & Schuster, Sydney, 1989

Reck, Ross R., Ph.D. and Long, Brian G., Ph.D., *The Win-Win Negotiator*, Blanchard Training and Development, Inc., Escondido, 1985

Restack, Richard M., M.D., *The Brain, The Last Frontier*, Warner Books, New York, 1979

Restack, Richard M., M.D., *The Mind*, Bantam Books, New York, 1988

Robbins, Anthony, *Unlimited Power*, Simon and Schuster, London, 1986

Sheehy, Gail, *Passages*, Bantam Books, New York, 1976

Sher, Barbara and Gottlieb, Annie, *Wishcraft, How To Get What You Really Want*, The Viking Press, New York, 1979

Silva, Jose and Miele, Philip, *The Silva Mind Control Method*, Simon and Schuster Inc., New York, 1977

Silver, Susan, *Organized To Be The Best!*, Adams-Hall Publishing, Los Angeles, 1989

Stearn, Jess, *The Power of Alpha Thinking*, William Morrow and Company, New York, 1976

Townsend, Robert, *Up the Organization*, Alfred A. Knopf, New York, 1970

Tracy, Brian, *The Psychology of Achievement*, (cassette tape set), Nightingale-Conant Corporation, Chicago

Trump, Donald J. and Schwartz, Tony, *The Art of The Deal*, Warner Books, New York, 1989

Viscott, David, Dr, *The Language of Feelings*, Morrow and Company, New York, 1983

Waitley, Denis, *Being the Best*, Pocket Books, New York, 1987

Ziglar, Zig, *See You At The Top*, Pelican Publishing Company, Louisiana, 1984

INDEX

The author gratefully acknowledges Random House Inc., Alfred Knopf Inc., New York, for permission to use the extract on page 13 from *The Art of the Deal* by Donald Trump with Tony Schwartz.